W9-CCH-651

Elizabeth Taylor

1932 – 2011

For Mel and Peter Davenport

With Love

Published in 2011 by André Deutsch
An imprint of the Carlton Publishing Group
20 Mortimer Street
London W1T 3JW

10 9 8 7 6 5 4 3 2 1

Text © André Deutsch 2011
Design © André Deutsch 2011

All rights reserved. This book is sold subject to the condition that it
may not be reproduced, stored in a retrieval system or transmitted
in any form or by any means, electronic, mechanical, photocopying,
recording or otherwise without the publisher's prior consent.

A CIP catalogue record for this book is available from the British
Library.

ISBN 978 0 233 00341 2

Printed in Dubai

Elizabeth Taylor

1932 – 2011

QUEEN OF THE SILVER SCREEN

IAN LLOYD

ANDRE
DEUTSCH

BOCA RATON PUBLIC LIBRARY
BOCA RATON, FLORIDA

Contents

Introduction

"I'm a survivor – a living example of what people can go through and survive."

RIGHT *Elizabeth Taylor in all her beauty in a promotional shot for the film* Elephant Walk *(1954).*

$\mathcal{E}$lizabeth Taylor led more than one life, offering her charmed public a series of different identities. Fame is often transitory, but a film about a horse, *National Velvet,* propelled her to international renown in 1944, and her film career, beauty, marriages, charity work, love of expensive jewellery and never-ending battle with health ensured she stayed in the public consciousness for the rest of her days.

As a movie actress she was feted, nominated five times for best actress at the Academy Awards and winning twice, for *BUtterfield 8* and *Who's Afraid of Virginia Woolf?*. She was directed by, among others, John Huston, Joseph L Mankiewicz, George Cukor, Vincente Minnelli and Franco Zeffirelli. She was one of the finest interpreters of the challenging works of Tennessee Williams and Edward Albee. When her film career took a nosedive in the 1970s, she reinvented herself as a stage actress, appearing on Broadway and in London in *The Little Foxes* and starring alongside Richard Burton in *Private Lives.*

Taylor had a talent for reinvention. Just when we thought she was in danger of fading from public awareness she would bounce back. After a battle against the bottle and her ever-fluctuating weight in the

LEFT *Elizabeth the child star. A scene from* National Velvet *(1944), the movie in which the 12-year-old first captured viewers' hearts, showing the acting skills and star qualities that would endure throughout her life.*

1970s, she emerged trim in the mid-'80s. After another battle against prescription drugs and alcohol, she emerged yet again victorious in the early '90s.

She was one of the few celebrities whose first name was instantly recognizable the world over, and "Liz to Marry Again" or "Liz in Hospital" were headlines we grew accustomed to over the years, In 1992 the very fact that she had arrived at Heathrow, prior to attending a Freddie Mercury tribute concert, was enough to make the BBC lunchtime news. Her arrival at Wembley Stadium for the same event ensured a standing ovation. Even at 60, she could rock the crowds.

When most of Hollywood was steering clear of the developing AIDS crisis, Taylor relished the challenge of making the world aware of its impact, especially after the deaths of her close friends Rock Hudson and the designer Halston. She even established her own AIDS charity.

Her own private life was a roller-coaster of emotion, with eight marriages to seven men, including two she referred to as the loves of her life: Mike Todd and Richard Burton. Her marriage to the latter was her longest and as "the Burtons" they were an integral part of the '60s jet set. Having scandalized society by openly flaunting their love affair, they ended the decade as friends of Princess Margaret, Princess Grace and the Duke and Duchess of Windsor, as well as reigning as Hollywood royalty in their own right.

In the chapter of this book covering the relationship of "Liz and Dick" there are exclusive photos of the couple's private life together. We see Taylor the wife, enjoying lazy days with Burton by the pool; Taylor the mother, very much hands-on and having fun; Taylor the joker – acting up for the camera in her kitchen; and Taylor the friend – partying with Marlon Brando and others.

Taylor was the ultimate survivor. Her last years were a constant battle against ill health; yet even when, as she admitted to her fellow Dame, Julie Andrews, "I'm falling to bits," she was still an inspiration, and showed the world her zest for life was undiminished. Asked once to sum up her personal philosophy, her answer was pure Elizabeth Taylor: "When people say, 'She's got everything,' I've got one answer – I haven't had tomorrow."

ABOVE LEFT *Elizabeth the wife and lover: Taylor and Burton on holiday, relaxing by a swimming pool, c.1967, during the years of their intense, stormy yet undeniably loving marriage (1964–74).*

ABOVE *Elizabeth the AIDS activist, speaking in 1992 at the concert in memory of Queen singer Freddie Mercury. Taylor showed the courage to speak out on the subject long before it was recognized in society at large.*

1

The Early Years

"*Mummy, I think I want to be an actress, a movie star!*"

RIGHT *Elizabeth Taylor, aged around six years old. This early photo hints at the star quality and photogenic looks that would lead her to being worshipped by movie audiences around the world.*

Elizabeth Rosemond Taylor was born on 27 February 1932 in Hampstead, London. To be precise, she entered the world at Heathwood, 8 Wildwood Road, NW11. Although she was born in England, her parents were both American, so Elizabeth was born with dual citizenship. When she married Welshman Richard Burton she applied to become a British citizen by choice, declaring: "It is not true that I love America less, but I love my husband more."

Throughout her life she was a frequent visitor to the land of her birth, sweeping into the UK with a dozen suitcases, assorted staff, bodyguards, pets, husbands and children, and would nearly always base herself at her favourite hotel – London's Dorchester – and in her favourite suite, the Oliver Messel. Asked, at one of her regular airport press conferences, how it felt to be back in Britain, she said, "It's great, but don't forget I was born here!" Later, when she was made a Dame of the British Empire by Queen Elizabeth II in 2000, the equally stellar Elizabeth Taylor said, "It's the most exciting – and I do not exaggerate – day in my life."

The actress inherited family names – Elizabeth after both of her grandmothers and Rosemond as a reminder of Granny Taylor's maiden name. Throughout her life she would hate the abbreviation so beloved of newspaper mastheads the world over: Liz. "People who know me and hope to know me better certainly do not call me Liz," she once commented, "They call me Elizabeth."

Elizabeth's father, Francis Taylor, was a moderately successful art dealer. Her mother, Sara Warnbrodt, enjoyed a brief theatrical career under the name Sara Sothern. Their only daughter would knock both their careers into the outer stratosphere, receiving the ultimate acting accolade of being a double Oscar winner and, as a discerning art collector, amassing works

LEFT *A portrait of Elizabeth Taylor as a child, taken in the mid-1930s. She would later describe her early years in England as the "happiest days of her childhood".*

BELOW *Elizabeth Taylor's birthplace and childhood home, "Heathwood", in Hampstead Garden Suburb, north London. Designed by architect Matthew Dawson in 1926, the Georgian-style house boasted six bedrooms, servant's quarters and a tennis court. Prior to the arrival of the Taylors, it had been the home of the artist Augustus John. In 2008 "Heathwood" was put up for sale for the first time in 30 years, at an asking price of UK£6.5 million.*

by Renoir, van Gogh, Degas, Monet, Mondigliani and Utrillo, to name but a few.

Francis and Sara also had a son, named Howard after his great-uncle, who was born in June 1929. He would share his sister's dazzling looks, having inherited the same well-defined features and fabulous eyes.

Baby Elizabeth was born with residual hypertrichosis, giving her excessive hair. Her mother recalled in a 1954 article for *McCalls*: "As the precious bundle was placed in my arms, my heart stood still. There, inside the cashmere shawl, was the *funniest* looking baby I had ever seen! Her hair was long and black. Her ears were covered with thick black fuzz and inlaid into the side of her head: her nose looked like a top-tilted button, and her tiny face was so tightly closed it looked as if it would never unfold."

Thankfully the condition proved a temporary one, though her mother later recollected being informed that her daughter had an even rarer one: "The doctor told us she had a mutation. Well that sounded just awful – *a mutation*. But, when he explained her eyes had double rows of eyelashes, I thought, well, now, that doesn't sound so terrible at all."

Elizabeth would remember her six years in London as "the happiest days of my childhood". The family was moderately well off thanks to Francis's stake in the Howard Young Gallery in Bond Street. Young was Francis

ABOVE *A family portrait from the 1930s, featuring (left to right) Elizabeth, her mother Sara and her brother Howard. Sara enjoyed a short-lived career on the stage that led her to invest a great deal of effort in building her daughter's stellar success.*

RIGHT *A young Elizabeth poses for a picture with a four-legged friend. In just a few years, her role as a young jockey in* National Velvet *(1944) would catapult her to stardom.*

Taylor's uncle. He and Victor Cazalet, a wealthy art collector and MP who befriended Sara and her family, were both benefactors to the young family. Cazalet is said to have paid for Elizabeth and Howard's education.

The future actress attended the Byron House School in Highgate, north London. "She wasn't an outstanding pupil, but she had such charm," recalled one of her teachers, Mary Mason.

A problem for Taylor's biographers is that publicists at her studio, MGM, would richly embroider the biographies of all its stars. Elizabeth was no exception, and her childhood in London was rewritten as an aristocratic idyll in which she mixed with royalty on a regular basis. She never performed before the king, as has been claimed, but she certainly performed, at the Vacani Dance School, for the young princesses Elizabeth and Margaret, accompanied by their mother, the Duchess of York, at a charity fund raiser. In her memoirs written in 1963, the actress traced her love of the stage and entertainment to that royal gala performance. "It was a marvellous moment," she wrote. "The isolation, the hugeness, the feeling of space and no end to space, the lights, the music – and then the applause bringing you back into focus, the noise rattling against your face."

By the spring of 1939, it was felt that war with Germany was becoming increasingly likely and Sara insisted the family should move to California. Howard Young's decision to sell the London art gallery proved the deciding factor.

On 3 April, Sara, Howard and Elizabeth sailed to the United States on the SS *Manhattan*, while Francis remained in London to close the business. Legend has it that during the eight-day voyage, the Taylors enjoyed a screening of *The Little Princess*, starring Hollywood's favourite child actor, Shirley Temple. As the credits faded, seven-year-old Elizabeth turned to Sara and whispered, "Mummy, I think I want to be an *actress*. A movie star!" That was the MGM version of things. Taylor herself once put it more bluntly: "I never wanted a career – it was forced on me."

RIGHT *Shirley Temple as a scullery maid in* The Little Princess *(1938). According to legend, Temple's performance had a huge impact on the young Elizabeth and influenced her desire to be an actress.*

2

Adolescence & a Grand National Winner

"I want it all quickly, 'cause I don't want God to stop and think and wonder if I'm getting more than my fair share."

As Velvet Brown in *National Velvet*

RIGHT *An official studio portrait of the young star-in-the-making, taken during the shooting of* National Velvet *(1944).*

A year after the Taylors arrived in California, Victor Cazalet gave Sara a letter of introduction to his friend, the gossip columnist Hedda Hopper. The two women arranged to meet and Elizabeth was taken along to literally sing for her supper.

Years later Hopper recalled the eight-year-old as "innocent and lovely as a day in spring. I liked and pitied her from the start, when her mother, bursting with ambition, brought her to my house." The influential journalist spotted Sara's motives straightaway. Mrs Taylor was clearly using her daughter to recreate her own frustrated career. "She had never gotten over Broadway," wrote Hopper. "She wanted to have a glamorous life again through her child."

Meanwhile Francis Taylor had established an art gallery at the Beverley Hills Hotel on Sunset Boulevard, where it soon attracted a high-class clientele including employees from the film studios and their families. One such was wife of J. Cheever Cowdin, the chairman of Universal Pictures. Mrs Cowdin happened to be visiting one day when Sara and Elizabeth were in the gallery. The quick-thinking and ambitious Sara invited the Cowdins for tea; and of course Elizabeth, now aged nine, was shown off to the studio chief.

Sara's tactics worked. Elizabeth was signed up for Universal on 21 April 1941, and by the end of the summer began work on *There's One Born Every Minute* in which she was woefully miscast as a charmless brat who, Taylor recalled later, "had to shoot rubber bands at ladies' bottoms".

BELOW *Courage of Lassie (1946) was 14-year-old Elizabeth Taylor's second film featuring the canine heroine. Her role as Priscilla in the previous movie,* Lassie Come Home (1943), *had been a minor character, but now she received the first top billing of her career.*

ABOVE *In her movie debut, nine-year-old Elizabeth Taylor was cast as an obnoxious child playing opposite Carl Switzer in the Universal Pictures film* There's One Born Every Minute *(1942). It was to be her only film for Universal – she was fired by the studio a year later.*

The studio was unimpressed with her performance and cancelled the contract. Elizabeth's fledgling career was put on hold until the summer of 1942 when, in another remarkable coincidence (or MGM rewriting of history), Francis Taylor was on air-raid duty one night in Beverley Hills with Samuel Marx, a neighbour and also a producer for Metro.

Marx admitted he was having problems finding a suitable girl with an English accent to star alongside another child star, Roddy McDowall, in *Lassie Come Home,* which was due to begin filming that autumn. McDowall, four years Elizabeth's senior, was also born in London, and would become one of the actress's closest friends.

In an interview recorded in 2000, Taylor recalled her screen test: "I went out and I just got on with it: 'poor Lassie, poor girl' and I got the part and I did my segment in two weeks. They then signed me up for 18 years!"

Elizabeth was a natural actress. "I had a great imagination," she once said, "I just slid into it, and it was like a piece of cake."

Her next role was a bit part in *Jane Eyre,* playing pious Helen Burns who suffers a tragic death from consumption at Lowood School early on in the film.

As her film career took off, Taylor's own childhood petered out. "How come I missed so much?" she queried later. "When was I ever a child?"

Her schooling was lamentable: "As far as education went on the set, they would have a little black cubby hole," she recalled half a century later. "You would have your tutor and the minimum you could be in there was ten minutes; so you had to ram some facts into your mind, go out on set, do your lines, come back, pick up where you'd left off, go out, slip back into character. It was not easy. I don't know why we weren't all a bunch of

ABOVE *Taylor's brief appearance in* Jane Eyre *(1944) as the tragic character Helen Burns was an uncredited minor role. She is shown here with Peggy Ann Garner, who played Jane Eyre as a child.*

RIGHT *Despite her youth, Taylor's beautiful eyes – a deep blue that appeared violet – gave the impression of an old soul in a young body. According to the biographer Alexander Walker, her casting director at Universal complained that "her eyes are too old, she doesn't have the face of a child". In later years, this quality would be a great asset in her acting career.*

OPPOSITE *In the movie* The White Cliffs of Dover *(1944) Taylor played a small role as farmer's daughter Betsey Kenney. Here, here in an on-set geography lesson, she directs the class's attention to the west coast of the USA. This wartime film also featured fellow child star – and lifelong friend – Roddy McDowall, with whom Taylor had appeared in* Lassie Come Home *(1943).*

LEFT *Aged 17, Elizabeth Taylor chats with supposed "girl friends" before receiving her graduation diploma from University High School, Los Angeles on 26 January 1950. The publicity photo was designed to present the actress as a model student, but in fact she had never attended the school and received only a limited education at the MGM studio school. In later years she bemoaned her lack of formal education.*

schizophrenics – well a lot of us were."

Thanks to MGM make-believe, the outside world saw Taylor as a model student. Photographers captured her surrounded by books and papers, and in January 1950 the studio staged a graduation ceremony for her, complete with cap and gown, at a school she had never attended, surrounded by classmates she had never met.

In 1944 Taylor starred opposite Mickey Rooney in *National Velvet*, the role that would catapult the 12-year-old actress to international stardom. She played Velvet Brown, who is given a wild but gifted horse called Pie, whom she decides to train for the Grand National – England's premier National Hunt race – in which, disguised as a boy, she would ride him to victory.

Angela Lansbury, another British-born star, now best known for her starring role in the US detective series *Murder She Wrote*, played Velvet's older sister, Edwina. She later recalled "being, even at that time, dazzled by her colouring which was so extraordinary, the violet blue eyes, and the dark hair, the freckles, the natural look in her cheeks. She was the most glamorous little girl I had ever seen."

Taylor's violet eyes were to be a talking point throughout her life. Film critic David Stratton wrote, "I was ushered into her presence at the official reception and found myself transfixed by her famous violet eyes. I have never seen eyes of that colour before or since, and I don't believe cinemagoers were able to appreciate how remarkable they were." Taylor herself once commented, "They are not violet as publicized but different colours depending on what I wear."

OPPOSITE *On the set of* National Velvet *(1944), an exuberant Taylor takes directions from above as the camera crew set up for the next sequence. Having ridden since the age of four, she did her own riding and many of her own stunts for the movie, but a fall from a horse while filming left her with back problems that would plague her for the rest of her life.*

LEFT, ABOVE *At an MGM production photo shoot, 12-year-old Elizabeth Taylor tries on a costume.*

LEFT *Racing towards stardom, this Technicolor still shows Taylor as junior jockey Velvet Brown on her faithful steed, Pie, from* National Velvet *(1944).*

LEFT *Elizabeth Taylor's involvement in charity work began early in her career. She is pictured here with Franklin D. Roosevelt Jr and Mrs Harry S. (Bess) Truman in January 1946 in Washington, DC during a CBS radio broadcast for the March of Dimes, a charity organization whose mission is to protect the health of infants.*

RIGHT *Pictured at Southampton docks in England in 1947 are 16-year-old Elizabeth Taylor and her mother, Sara. Her mother's relentless championing of Elizabeth in Hollywood had achieved its goal, and Taylor revisited her country of birth as a famous movie star.*

After the success of *National Velvet*, Taylor was cast in another animal film, *Courage of Lassie*. Most of her other adolescent films – *Life With Father* (for Warner Brothers), *A Date With Judy* and *Julia Misbehaves*, were popular in their day but are largely forgotten now. The decade ended with her role as the snooty Amy in *Little Women*, complete with an unflattering strawberry-blonde wig. Her later comment on the part, "I liked playing the role of a young girl in love," is a reminder that Taylor's real love life was in its embryonic stages and would soon find her on a path that would prove to be rockier and more eventful than any script writer could ever devise.

It was MGM rather than Mother Nature that decided that Taylor was ready to court the opposite sex. The studio set her up with a handsome auburn-haired football player, an all-American youth, Glenn Davis, who had just graduated from West Point. For Sara, who had masterminded her daughter's career, it seemed Elizabeth's love life was a similar done deal. "When I saw that frank, wonderful face," Sara wrote of Davis, "I thought, 'This is the Boy.' I felt such a sense of relief." Mrs Taylor lived to the ripe age of 98 and probably grew used to feeling a sense of relief every time her daughter brought home "the right one".

Davis eventually left to fight in Korea but not before presenting Elizabeth with her first gift of jewellery, a necklace made up of 69 cultured pearls. In March 1949, another more serious affair began when she was introduced to the wealthy, dark-haired William Pawley, at a dinner party at the home of her great-uncle Howard Young at Star Island, Florida.

At 28, Pawley was more than ten years older than Elizabeth. Besides

OPPOSITE *A trio of MGM starlets –
Janet Leigh, June Allyson and Elizabeth
Taylor – enjoying a singalong during
the making of* Little Women *(1949).*

LEFT *Elizabeth captivates a trio of
canine fans, c.1947. A lifelong dog lover
with a particular fondess for Pekineses
and Malteses, she was once quoted as
saying, "Some of my best leading men
have been dogs and horses."*

BELOW *A blonde-wigged Taylor (right)
as Amy, the vain third March sister,
in MGM's adaptation of Louisa May
Alcott's* Little Women *(1949). Amy is
wearing a clothespeg on her nose to
straighten it. On the left is Margaret
O'Brien as Amy's younger sister, Beth,
differing from the original novel, in
which Beth is a year older than Amy.*

being extremely handsome and rich, he was also debonair, charming and witty, and 17-year-old Taylor fell headlong in love.

Meanwhile Davis flew down to Florida with an engagement ring for his intended. Elizabeth acted the part of besotted girlfriend, greeting her hero beau in front of the MGM-orchestrated press call. Privately, however, she was cold and indifferent, and Davis returned to Los Angeles hurt and confused by the situation. He did figure in Elizabeth's life one final time, later the same month, when, for what reason we will never know, he acquiesced to the studio's suggestion that he should accompany her to that year's Academy Awards ceremony.

Meanwhile Pawley and Taylor grew closer, and in May 1949 he presented her with a substantial $16,000-dollar three-and-a-half-carat emerald-cut solitaire diamond ring. MGM organized another photocall, at which Taylor declared her ring "a nice piece of ice".

The engagement petered out, and finally broke altogether, following Pawley's insistence that she should abandon her film career to be with him. Taylor, with two more movie projects on the horizon, flatly refused.

Their romance hit the headlines one more time following Taylor's death. In early April it was announced that 66 love letters written by the 17-year-old actress to Pawley were to be auctioned off the following month. Unsurprisingly they are both vivid and incredibly passionate: "I've never loved anyone in my life before one third as much as I love you – and I never will (well, as far as that goes – I'll never love anyone else – period)."

She also turned down the blandishments of the massively wealthy but increasingly eccentric Howard Hughes, who offered to buy her her own film studio if she married him. Sara was euphoric: "I feel as if I am dreaming." Elizabeth, on the other hand, was appalled, and told her mother, "I don't want anything to do with him. I don't care how much money he has."

By now the star was becoming increasingly tired of her mother's meddling, and said of her around this time, "She's a large pain in the ass." This was, after all, the same girl who, three years earlier at the age of 14, told MGM's god-like boss, Louis B Mayer, "You and your studio can just go to hell." Aged 17, Taylor was proving she was more than able to stand up for herself against suitors, studio chiefs and, at long last, her overly ambitious mother.

OPPOSITE *Taylor with her MGM-approved boyfriend, Lt Glenn Davis of West Point. They are pictured here on 24 March 1949, arriving at the Academy Awards ceremony in Hollywood.*

LEFT *Moving on from her brief relationship with Glenn Davis, Taylor poses with her fiancé William D. Pawley Jnr at his father's home in Florida on 7 June 1949. Taylor later called off the engagement due to Pawley's insistence that she give up her movie career after their marriage.*

3

Marriage, Motherhood & Monty Clift

" I fell off my pink cloud with a thud."

RIGHT *Elizabeth Taylor in 1951. While her marriage to Conrad Hilton was effectively over and her private life was at a very low ebb, her screen career was about to reach dizzy new heights.*

In 1949, 17-year-old Elizabeth Taylor was dubbed "the most eligible actress in Hollywood". By 1957 she had been married twice, divorced twice, and was the mother of two young sons.

The early 1950s were also significant in her development as an actress. Unlike many child actors, Taylor managed the transition to adult roles with complete ease. Ending one decade playing sassy teenaged Amy in *Little Women*, she began the next one playing the wife of 38-year-old Robert Taylor in *Conspirator*. The movie bombed at the box office but *Variety* declared "she came out with flying colours".

Elizabeth's next role was in *Father of the Bride*, as Kay Banks, bride-to-be of the gloriously named Buckley Dunstan. It was a romp of a film, in which Spencer Tracy, playing Taylor's father Stanley, effortlessly steals scene after scene as he tries to cope with the mayhem that unravels in the weeks between Kay's engagement and wedding.

As so often happened in Elizabeth's life, reality and Hollywood make-believe were almost interchangeable. Towards the end of 1949 she met and swiftly fell in love with Conrad Nicholas Hilton – known as Nicky – the 23-year-old heir of Conrad Snr, who had recently divorced the actress Zsa Zsa Gabor. Nicky was the great-uncle of the twenty-first-century socialites Paris and Nicky Hilton.

The new man in Elizabeth's life was an irresponsible playboy who led a directionless life career-wise, and instead enjoyed a hedonistic lifestyle among the Hollywood elite. He once declared: "The trouble with me is I have a millionaire father."

OPPOSITE *Elizabeth played her first adult role as the wife of Robert Taylor in the film* Conspirator. *Although the film bombed at the box office, her performance was well reviewed.*

LEFT *Elizabeth Taylor walking down the aisle with her on-screen father, played by Spencer Tracy, in* Father of the Bride. *In a clever PR exercise, the film was released two weeks after her real-life wedding to Conrad Hilton.*

Hilton had charm in abundance and easily won over Sara. She declared that Elizabeth "never accepted invitations or made dates until the young men had been at our house and met with our approval". Had she known that her daughter's beau was a drunkard and gambler, she might not have been so fulsome in her praise.

On 21 February 1950, six days before Elizabeth's eighteenth birthday, the Taylors announced their daughter's engagement, literally hours after shooting had ended on *Father of the Bride*. MGM, capitalizing on this public-relations dream, decided to release the movie two weeks after the actual wedding at the Church of the Good Shepherd, off Santa Monica Boulevard, on 6 May. Helen Rose, who dressed Taylor at MGM, produced a near-identical wedding dress to the one worn by Elizabeth in the film, and the studio supplied everything else from the flowers to the attendants' outfits.

On the morning of her special day, Elizabeth's previous fiancé, William Pawley, turned up at the Taylor family home, and spent 15 minutes with the bride-to-be before rushing out of the house, leaving her in tears. She pulled herself together in time for the ceremony and later recalled: "I closed my eyes to any problems and walked radiantly down the aisle."

Outside the church there was a melee of police, press and public. It turned out to be the prototype for the chaos that would typify most of Taylor's subsequent weddings.

A few days later the Hiltons boarded the *Queen Mary* at the start of a three-month cruise. Elizabeth took with her 17 suitcases and a maid. It was just as well to have a friendly face to hand, as Nicky spent most of the cruise and their time in Monte Carlo either drinking or gambling.

ABOVE *Elizabeth arriving in Mexico from New York, with fiancé Conrad Hilton, son of the wealthy hotel-chain owner, and her mother Sara Taylor. The couple had recently become engaged.*

"Then came disillusionment," wrote Elizabeth years later, "rude and brutal. I fell off my pink cloud with a thud."

Taylor maintained a dignified silence on her first marriage until Hilton died from a heart attack at the age of 42, brought on by years of alcohol abuse. Elizabeth finally revealed to the world that Hilton was a wife beater. "He became sullen, angry and abusive, physically and mentally. The marriage scarred me and left me with horrible memories." The final beating caused a miscarriage, which she recounted in vivid detail many years later: "I left him after having the baby kicked out of my stomach. I had terrible pains. I saw the baby in the toilet." She had no idea she was having a baby, and so Hilton would have had no idea of what could ensue when he hit her. She used this as a mitigating excuse for his actions, which she blamed on his drinking.

For his part, Hilton found marriage to one of the most famous women in the world was far from easy, with photographers and fans swamping their every public appearance. "I didn't marry a girl," he said later, "I married an institution."

The MGM machine which had choreographed Elizabeth's wedding now sprung into action to protectively shield one of its most lucrative stars. A studio publicity release issued on behalf of Elizabeth broke the news: "Nicky and I have come to a final parting of the ways. There is no possibility of a reconciliation." Elizabeth filed for divorce on 22 December 1950, on the grounds of "extreme mental cruelty". The union was dissolved on 29 January 1952. Marriage number one was over after just nine months.

While Taylor's private life was suffering, her screen career was about to hit one of its all-time highs. In late 1949, around the time her romance with

ABOVE *Wearing a stunning $1,500 satin gown – a wedding gift from MGM studios – Taylor is pictured here with her first husband, Nicky Hilton, outside the church shortly after their wedding on 6 May 1950.*

Hilton was taking root, Elizabeth began filming *A Place in the Sun,* directed by George Stevens and based on Theodore Dreiser's novel *An American Tragedy.* The film was scheduled for release in 1950 but was shelved for another year. partly to avoid a clash with the much-hyped blockbuster *Sunset Boulevard* which was widely tipped to be a triumph at the Oscars. (The delay allowed Stevens to spend some worthwhile time editing the film, which in the end won six Oscars, including one for Stevens himself. *Boulevard* won just three the previous year, despite receiving 11 nominations.)

Taylor later revealed that her role as society girl Angela Vickers, playing opposite Montgomery Clift as George Eastman, caused her to re-evaluate her acting style. She had always relied on her instinctive approach whereas "Monty" was a disciple of method acting.

Fifty years after filming this iconic movie, Taylor stated, *"A Place in the Sun* is one of my favourite films." The teenaged star soon realized her childish behaviour was at odds with her co-star's intense approach. "I still would camp around on the set and drive everyone mad… but when I saw Monty preparing I thought, 'My God, it isn't all about having fun,' and I think that's when I first looked at him and saw how involved he was."

Taylor and Clift shared an emotional quality in their acting, but off screen Elizabeth also developed the nurturing style she would adopt later on with both her co-stars and her husbands, especially Richard Burton. She had an innate desire to comfort and mother anyone who was at all vulnerable, and Clift, who was addicted to alcohol and prescription drugs as well as a closet gay, was the first of a long list of damaged creatures she was drawn to. Much as she was intrigued by his method acting, she was also aware of the dangers it could inflict on a sensitive character like his.

"I used to take Monty and say, 'Don't do this to yourself, you've got to release it when the scene's over,' and I'd hold him. I was only 17 on the film and it was sometimes like I was older than he was."

Shelley Winters, who played Taylor's rival for Monty's character in the film, recalled in 1985: *"A Place in the Sun* was the best thing she [Taylor] ever did. Elizabeth had a depth and simpleness which were really remarkable."

Elizabeth and Monty became friends off screen as well and, in May 1956, while driving home from a party at Taylor's house, Clift suffered horrific injuries when his car swerved off the road and hit a lamppost. "Leaving my house he had the worst accident I've ever seen," Taylor recalled 45 years later. "I was the first on the scene and pulled his head off the steering wheel. I probably shouldn't have touched him." Clift's head swelled following the impact and Taylor noticed his eyes were full of blood.

"He tried to say something and I said, 'What is it my love; what is it baby?' Finally I made out: 'Could you pull my teeth out?'" Two of the actor's teeth had pierced through his tongue and Taylor pulled them out for him. It must have been a horrific ordeal for both of them. The ambulance was 45 minutes late and, not surprisingly, she later reflected "it was a nightmare".

Following the collapse of her marriage to Hilton, Taylor dated several of her Hollywood contemporaries including the cinematographer Stanley Donen. It was while filming *Ivanhoe* in England that she fell under the spell of Michael Wilding, a handsome and popular matinee idol, some 20 years her senior.

Wilding was the archetypal English gentleman – cultured, sophisticated and the complete antithesis of Nicky Hilton. For Taylor it must have seemed like entering calm waters after a particularly choppy sea. The actress decided Wilding would not only be an ideal husband but an ideal father to the children she so desperately craved.

OPPOSITE *Elizabeth with Stanley Donen, one of the many men she dated after her first divorce.*

After her return to California, Wilding flew out to visit in December 1951. During a dinner at Romanoff's in Los Angeles, Taylor asked him to marry her. Wilding had produced a sapphire and diamond ring that he intended as a gift of friendship. "I reached for her right hand," he later recalled, "but she snatched it away, putting it on her left hand and waggling her third finger. 'That's where it belongs,' she said." Having admired the ring, she kissed her dinner date, and asked, "Dear shilly-shally, will you marry me?"

"Shilly-shally" appears to have had little choice once Taylor set her cap at him. They were married in a ten-minute ceremony at London's Caxton Hall on 21 February 1952, when the British capital was still subdued following the funeral of King George VI six days earlier. Despite this, a crowd of over a thousand blocked the streets around the registry office. A journalist who fought through the melee managed to ask Taylor how she felt about the 21-year age gap: the actress replied confidently, "Michael's just a child at heart."

ABOVE *Their marriage over after 205 days, Taylor and property heir Hilton met to discuss the details of their divorce settlement. Nicky planned to marry new fiancée Betsy von Furstenberg as soon as the annulment proceedings were finalized.*

Less than a year later, Elizabeth gave birth to Michael Howard Wilding, on 6 January 1953 following an emergency caesarean section. His brother Christopher Edward Wilding was born using the same procedure on their mother's twenty-third birthday, 27 February 1955.

Meanwhile, for a creature as volatile as Taylor, marriage to someone with a temperament as equable as Wilding's was bound to lead to problems. Having dumped one husband because of his physical abuse, she practically demanded it from her current one. A typical example was the day she snatched his newspaper off him and threw it into the fire after his tranquil crossword-filling got on her nerves. "So much for you and your games," she screamed. "Go on and hit me, why don't you?"

"I've never gone in for hitting hysterical females," Wilding replied completely calmly.

"Oh God," she moaned, "if only you would! At least that would prove you are flesh and blood instead of a stuffed dummy."

ABOVE *Elizabeth kisses Judy Garland good luck in her vaudeville performance during a backstage visit at New York's Palace theatre. Her escort for the night was good friend and co-star Montgomery Clift, seen here on the right.*

LEFT *Taylor and Montgomery Clift became lifelong friends on the set of* A Place in the Sun.

RIGHT *Clift and Taylor keeping warm on the set of* A Place in the Sun. *Elizabeth was drawn to sensitive people like Monty – an alcoholic, drug addict and closet homosexual – and the two became close friends off screen.*

BELOW *Clift and Taylor in a scene from* A Place in the Sun.

LEFT *Elizabeth strikes a convincing pin-up pose beside the pool in Hollywood, 1952.*

OPPOSITE *Taylor with Michael Wilding, a matinee idol 20 years her senior. The huge sapphire and diamond ring he gave her was intended as a token of friendship but Elizabeth slipped the ring on her wedding-ring finger and promptly proposed to him over dinner.*

In July 1956 MGM announced the demise of Taylor's second marriage. Her divorce was finalized the following January.

Elizabeth remained on cordial terms with the father of her two sons and gave him one of her more positive post-marital assessments: "He was one of the nicest people I had ever known. But I'm afraid in those last years I gave him rather a rough time, sort of hen-pecked him and probably wasn't mature enough for him." At the time of his sudden death in July 1979, she praised him as "a good father".

ABOVE *Police had to hold back the crowds as 3,000 fans gathered outside Caxton Hall, London, when Taylor and Wilding's 15-minute civil marriage ceremony took place in February 1952.*

ABOVE RIGHT *Taylor with her father Francis when he visited her on the set of* Love is Better Than Ever.

RIGHT *Taylor in 1952, watching her second husband Michael Wilding in the film* Trent's Last Case.

LEFT *6 January 1953. One of the first pictures of Elizabeth Taylor with her first son Michael Howard Wilding.*

RIGHT *Elizabeth and her son Michael Wilding Jnr, wearing matching bathing costumes.*

MELLOR

LEFT *Taylor on the set of* Giant *(1956) with James Dean. Once again she was drawn to this difficult and tortured soul and they became firm friends.*

RIGHT *Elizabeth became good friends with both her leading men in* Giant, *James Dean (left) and Rock Hudson (right). Unfortunately, they did not get on and she often found herself trying to soothe troubled waters between the two.*

BELOW *A policeman examines the wreckage of Montgomery Clift's car in Los Angeles after it crashed into a lamppost following a dinner party at Taylor and Wilding's house in 1956. Elizabeth was first on the scene of the horrific accident, in which Clift suffered serious head injuries.*

4

Numbers Three & Four

"Well, Mike's dead and I'm alive. What do you expect me to do – sleep alone?"

RIGHT *Taylor on the set of* Suddenly Last Summer.

The day after MGM announced Taylor's separation from Wilding, Mike Todd, the producer of *Around the World in 80 Days*, called to ask the actress to meet him at the studio. There he spent an hour telling her he loved her and wanted to marry her. Todd had tried to date her when she was married to Wilding, but Elizabeth, despite her multi-marriages, had some old-fashioned traits and wouldn't consider an affair. Now here he was pleading his case and refusing to take no for an answer.

"If this is was what getting swept off your feet was like," she commented later, "well, I must admit, as much of a brute as I thought he was, I was still quite flattered."

Shirley MacLaine, Taylor's fellow actress and friend, recalled: "Mike Todd was a steam-rolling fireball entrepreneur, impresario, who could talk you into anything." Born in 1909, he was the oldest of Taylor's husbands. The actress was in fact three years younger than his son, Mike Todd Jnr.

Mike and Elizabeth exchanged vows on 2 February 1957, when he was 47 and she was 24. This would be the only one of her eight marriages not to end in divorce. She later claimed he was one of the three loves of her life, alongside Richard Burton and jewellery. Todd was handsome, rakish, fun-loving and adventurous, and allowed Elizabeth to be spoiled, entertained and the willing recipient of more jewels than she'd ever had in her life.

In August the same year, Taylor gave birth to her third child, a daughter, Elizabeth Frances Todd, named after the actress and her father and soon to be known as Liza. While Taylor was still under sedation, doctors told Todd his wife should not have any more children and he agreed that a tubal ligation should be performed on her. Not surprisingly, when she came round

OPPOSITE *A pregnant Elizabeth Taylor returning home aboard the liner* Liberté *with husband Michael Todd. The couple laughed off rumours, sparked by public quarrels, that their five-month marriage was on the rocks.*

BELOW *Elizabeth Taylor with her husband, film producer Michael Todd, and family members following their civil wedding in Mexico in February 1957. Elizabeth had only left hospital a month earlier, having undergone spinal surgery the year before.*

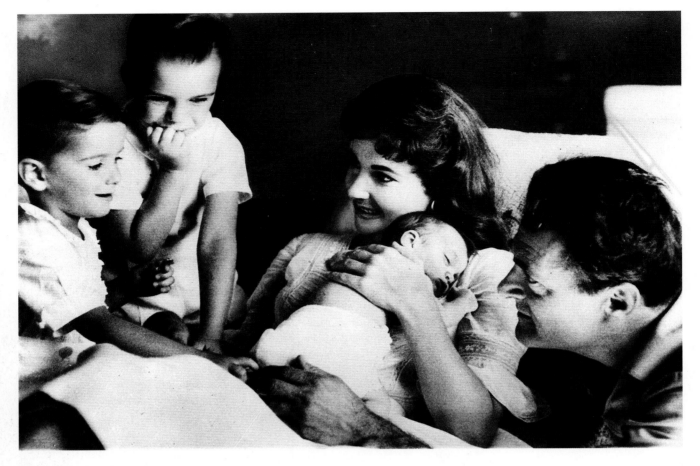

from the anaesthetic, Elizabeth was furious to discover what had happened to her and called it "a huge shock to me".

On 22 March 1958 Todd flew in his private jet *The Lucky Liz* to accept an award as Showman of the Year, to be presented by the Friars Club of New York at the Waldorf-Astoria Hotel. Taylor had been due to fly with him but a bout of pneumonia and a temperature of 103 degrees forced her to pull out.

She would later recount how Todd said goodbye to her five times. Every time he reached the door he rushed back to embrace her one more time.

Todd's aircraft hit a thunderstorm on its way to the east coast, crash landed and exploded. His body was burned beyond recognition and could only be identified because of his wedding ring, which was later sent to his widow. Taylor was told the news at 6am, when a secretary and her doctor entered her bedroom. Realizing immediately what must have happened, as they approached her bedside she screamed, "He's not! He's not!" She and Mike had been married for just 414 whirlwind days.

At the time of Todd's death, Elizabeth was filming one of her finest movies, *Cat on a Hot Tin Roof*, opposite Paul Newman. This would be the second of four films in a row for which she would be Oscar nominated: *Raintree County*, in which she again starred opposite Monty Clift, had earned her the first nomination in the spring of 1958. She would also be nominated for *Cat* in 1959, *Suddenly Last Summer* in 1960 and *BUtterfield 8* in 1961.

Taylor took just two weeks off, staying with her brother Howard and his wife, before resuming work on the film, based on the Tennessee Williams play. She would later recount how the trauma of her husband's death had left her with a stutter that for some reason disappeared the moment she

ABOVE *Elizabeth and Michael Todd pose for a family portrait with their newborn baby daughter Elizabeth Frances and Taylor's two sons from her second marriage, Christopher and Michael Wilding.*

RIGHT *A newly married Elizabeth Taylor with a duckling in her home, for* Person to Person *magazine in April 1957.*

slipped into a Southern accent.

Once again she found her instinctive style at odds with the intense method adopted by her co-star. Commentating on her approach, she told one interviewer: "The minute the camera goes on, something happens in me – then I start to pull out the stops, but when it's the rehearsal, my mind knows this is not the real thing."

Paul Newman was baffled by this and discussed it with the director Richard Brooks, asking, "Richard, is this it, is this all she's going to give?" Brooks reassured him: "It's ok Paul – you wait!"

Todd and Taylor's closest friends were the crooner Eddie Fisher and his wife, actress Debbie Reynolds. Fisher and Reynolds were clean-cut and as

OPPOSITE *Taylor in a scene from* Raintree County, *released in 1957.*

BELOW *Elizabeth suffered serious back injuries while the plane she was travelling in landed in Mexico. Here she is seen being placed on a stretcher before going to hospital as husband Michael Todd anxiously looks on.*

LEFT *Taylor and Todd board their plane in 1958. Just a short while later the plane would crash killing Todd and leaving Elizabeth a widow.*

BOTTOM LEFT *Elizabeth and her stepson Michael Todd Jnr arriving in Chicago for the funeral of her third husband Michael Todd, who died in a plane crash near Grants, New Mexico.*

OPPOSITE *Taylor in a scene from* Cat on a Hot Tin Roof, *directed by Richard Brook, and released in September, 1958.*

wholesomely American as cherry pie.

Fisher had hero-worshipped Mike and named his son Todd in honour of the impresario. Now he was by Elizabeth's side in her hour of need, and it wasn't too long before Taylor was kissing widowhood goodbye. On 29 August columnist Earl Wilson reported: "Elizabeth Taylor and Eddie Fisher were dancing it up at the Harwyn [nightclub] this morning, Eddie having been Mike Todd's close friend and now a sort of escort service for Liz."

The American media was firmly on the side of Debbie Reynolds, the wronged wife. In a 1959 interview she admitted her marriage had been in difficulty and that it was only a question of time before Fisher had some kind of fling: "I knew it would be someone, but I didn't believe it would be

Elizabeth." Never one to be daunted by the press, Taylor hosted a party for Fisher to help launch his new TV series. According to one columnist, she called it her "You-Can-All-Go-To-Hell Party". She also outraged Hedda Hopper by telling her, "Well, Mike's dead and I'm alive. What do you expect me to do – *sleep alone?*"

Coinciding with her new relationship, Taylor visited the Temple Israel in Hollywood, where she was accepted into the Jewish faith, adopting the name Elisheba Rachel. Judaism was Fisher's religion and also Todd's, though at the time the actress insisted her conversion was something she had wanted for a long time and wasn't motivated by her marriages. Any noteworthy action in Elizabeth's life automatically made headlines and when news of her change of faith broke, the Arab League banned the showing of her movies in every Arab country in the Middle East and Africa, although they would later rapidly backtrack when she starred as Cleopatra, Queen of the Nile.

Taylor married Fisher in May 1959 and the couple were soon starring in *BUtterfield 8*, one of Taylor's least-favourite movies. She claimed to have been made to do it by MGM "with a gun at my temple".

"I didn't speak to the director [Daniel Mann] for the whole of it." Once

OPPOSITE *Elizabeth Taylor with Paul Newman, Jack Carson, Madeleine Sherwood and Judith Anderson on the set of* Cat on a Hot Tin Roof *.*

BELOW *Taylor and Todd at the Derby in Epsom in June 1957, with friends Eddie Fisher and Debbie Reynolds following behind. The foursome were great friends and little did Debbie Reynolds know that soon Elizabeth would "steal" her husband from her.*

again she was at odds with method directing: "Everything was refer to this, refer to that." After the screening she mimicked her screen character, Gloria, who memorably wrote in lipstick "No Sale" across a mirror. In front of the production team, Taylor crossed to a studio mirror and wrote "Piece of S**t" in scarlet letters.

Taylor and Fisher's marriage lasted less than five years. When it ended acrimoniously in March 1964 she refused to talk about him, and thereafter he was one of the few topics that the normally forthright interviewee wouldn't let journalists mention. He died in September 2010 from complications following hip surgery. Taylor died six months and one day later. She may have chosen to forget her fourth husband, but she never forgot their shared faith. Her funeral was a private Jewish ceremony, presided over by Rabbi Jerry Cutler, and took place, in accordance with Jewish law, the day after her death.

LEFT, TOP *Elizabeth slipping out of the Blue Angel on East 55th Street, New York, where she and singer Eddie Fisher had spent a quiet hour together sipping champagne. When the couple heard that photographers were waiting outside, they left separately.*

LEFT *Eddie and Elizabeth rejoicing at the news that Eddie's wife Debbie Reynolds had agreed to a "quickie" divorce, leaving them free to marry. Elizabeth and Michael Todd had been close friends with the couple, and Eddie had comforted Elizabeth after Michael died.*

RIGHT *Taylor had recently been accepted into the Jewish faith, and so she and Fisher were married by two rabbis in Las Vegas on 12 May 1959 – 15 months after she was widowed when an air crash killed Michael Todd.*

LEFT *One of the most famous images of Taylor, from the film* Suddenly Last Summer. *The poster featured an illustration of the same image. Taylor earned another Oscar nomination for the film in which she co-starred with Katherine Hepburn and, once again, Montgomery Clift. Elizabeth stars as Catherine Holly, a young girl who witnesses the death of her cousin Sebastian on vacation and goes to pieces. Her dramatic monologue at the end of the film, in which she describes the murder, is unforgettable.*

RIGHT *Taylor boards a flight to Rome, where she would film* Cleopatra. *She appears to be wearing the $29^{7}/_{8}$-carat diamond engagement ring given to her by her third husband, Michael Todd.*

LEFT *As Gloria Wandrous in* BUtterfield 8. *Taylor hated the film, which was made under protest to fulfil a contractual obligation to MGM before being allowed to leave for 20th Century Fox to make* Cleopatra, *referring to it with Eddie Fisher as "Butterball Four". Once this scene was over, she scrawled an obscenity across the mirror.*

5

Cleopatra & the Love of Her Life

"I had to be with Richard. I knew it was wrong, I knew it would hurt people. I knew. I knew. But I also knew what I had to do. God help me, I had to be with Richard."

RIGHT *Elizabeth Taylor as Cleopatra. Her image has become synonymous with that of the Egyptian queen.*

he critical success of Taylor's roles in *Cat on a Hot Tin Roof* and *Suddenly Last Summer* made her the most bankable female star of the late 1950s.

She was an obvious choice to star in the Twentieth Century Fox epic *Cleopatra* and was signed up for the then record-breaking fee of $1 million. She demanded it be shot in Todd-AO, the widescreen film format developed by Mike Todd which she had inherited and would receive royalties for. She also owned a third of *Cleopatra* through her own production company, MCL Films, named after her children Mike, Chris and Liza. The film became famous for nearly bankrupting Fox, but its star walked away with a cool $7 million, as well as the man who would become the love of her life.

Filming began in England, at Pinewood Studios in Buckinghamshire, in September 1960, but Taylor had only made a handful of appearances before the camera when she contracted spinal meningitis. She was discharged after a week in hospital and promptly decamped to Palm Springs, California with Eddie Fisher and her children for a lengthy recuperation.

She returned to London the following March, and work on the film was about to resume when she collapsed at the Dorchester Hotel with a life-threatening bout of pneumonia. She was rushed to the London Clinic where an emergency tracheotomy was performed. Fisher was told his wife was dying, and when the news broke, thousands crowded the streets around the

BELOW *Taylor with her then husband Eddie Fisher (centre) and her children Christopher Wilding, Michael Wilding Jnr and Liza Todd at Bertram Mills's Circus, London, 1961. They were there with four other children to celebrate Michael's eighth birthday.*

ABOVE *Elizabeth leaving hospital in London following treatment for pneumonia, 23 March 1961. Her fame was such that, even in hospital, she couldn't escape her fans or the press.*

hospital. Taylor's fight for life soon became a global media story.

After a three-week stay in hospital, the actress once again returned to California, this time for a six-month recuperation, which she interrupted briefly in April to collect her Oscar as Best Actress for *BUtterfield 8,* which she later dubbed her "sympathy award".

Filming on *Cleopatra* resumed in September 1961, now relocated to Cinecitta studios outside Rome. Taylor made a Norma Desmond entrance in a full-length black mink coat with fussing acolytes bustling around her to dramatic effect. Director Joseph Mankiewicz kissed her hand in gentlemanly fashion and said, "My dear, you leave me breathless." "Of course I do," teased his leading lady.

Her recently appointed co-star, Richard Burton, stepped forward, but had Elizabeth expected another mellifluous compliment she was to be disillusioned pretty rapidly. "You're much too fat, luv," murmured Burton, adding, "but I have to admit you do have a pretty face." This was the sort of irreverence Taylor herself was prone to dishing out, and she roared with laughter. "Why, the nerve!" she shrieked with mock indignation. The meeting had an impact on the actor: "I will never forget that first laugh," he told a journalist much later.

Taylor and Burton had met years earlier at a Hollywood party thrown by the actor Stewart Granger and his then wife Jean Simmons. Richard attended with his wife Sybil and was soon reciting Shakespeare in his

booming Welsh voice. Elizabeth later recalled thinking, "My goodness, does the man ever shut up?" and she completely blanked him.

Now, on the set of *Cleopatra*, the attraction was mutual, and the couple soon fell into a pattern of lengthy lunches and late-night partying, to the dismay of the production team. With Eddie and Sybil dividing their time between Rome and home, neither was on hand to prevent the inevitable.

By the time Taylor and Burton were sharing their first scenes together in January 1962 they were also sharing a bed. Mankiewicz let his producer Walter Wanger in on the secret, telling him. "I've been sitting on a volcano all alone for too long, and I want to give you some facts you ought to know. Liz and Burton are not just *playing* Cleopatra and Antony."

The gossip columnist Louella Parsons, whom ironically Taylor would portray in the 1985 television movie *Malice in Wonderland*, broke the news that the actress's marriage was in trouble. Eddie Fisher hurried to Rome a few days later and his wife admitted the rumours were true.

Many years later, Elizabeth gave her own melodramatic account of the affair: "I had to be with Richard. I knew it was wrong, I knew it would hurt people. I knew. *I knew.* But I also knew what I had to do. God help me, I had to be with Richard."

Meanwhile Eddie Fisher had a meeting with Sybil Burton. The latter

OPPOSITE *Despite her hatred of the movie, her roll in* BUtterfield 8 *won her the Best Actress Oscar in 1961. Her response – "I still say it stinks."*

BELOW *Following a break in filming due to illness, filming on* Cleopatra *began again in September 1961. Elizabeth and Eddie decamped to Rome and are seen here being serenaded in their limousine outside a restaurant. Paparazzi followed Elizabeth everywhere she went.*

dismissed the affair as another of her husband's flings, telling the crooner, "He always comes back to me." Fisher's response was: "Clearly you don't know my wife," and explained that "anything Elizabeth wants, Elizabeth always gets".

A distraught Sybil reported the conversation to her husband, and the contrite, guilt-ridden actor decided to end the affair and return to his family. Taylor, unused to such rejection, took an overdose of sleeping tablets in a cry for help and was rushed to the Salvatore Mundi hospital to have her stomach pumped.

Elizabeth and Eddie Fisher announced they were divorcing on 2 April 1962. By then Taylor and Burton were once again an item and the paparazzi descended on Rome to snap what Burton called "Le Scandale".

The Italian press dubbed Taylor a marriage wrecker and the Pope himself condemned them. In an unequivocal stance, the Vatican radio station said: "We like to call Rome a Holy City. God forbid it becomes a city of perversion."

The Cinecitta studios received a bomb threat and Taylor was heckled on the way to the studio. She was due to film Cleopatra's entrance into Rome, and, in those pre-computer-generated-imagery days, this necessitated thousands of extras. The actress feared she would be booed or even shot at, but the crowd which had been primed to chant "Cleopatra! Cleopatra! Cleopatra!" eventually changed the wording to "Leez! Leez! Leez!".

OPPOSITE *Taylor on the* Cleopatra *set with director Joseph Mankiewicz. She negotiated a staggering $1 million deal to make the film, a record at the time, and actually made $7 million due to shrewd investment in it.*

BELOW *Elizabeth in a Roman nightclub with husband Eddie Fisher, and future husband Richard Burton.*

Elizabeth was greatly moved by the display of affection from the Italian extras. "The tears were pouring down my face," she recalled later. Richard stood by, clearly mesmerized by the effect his lover had on the crowd.

In June 1962 Taylor filmed her last scenes in *Cleopatra* and her lengthy sojourn in Italy came to an end. The film opened exactly a year later and was panned by the critics for Mankiewicz's bad script, as well as the movie's interminable length and often-wooden performances. Elizabeth received the worst reviews of her career and was devastated.

Meanwhile, two months after leaving Italy, Richard had moved into Elizabeth's 16-room chalet in Gstaad in Switzerland. Now, back in the real world, the actress had time to reconsider their relationship. After one spectacular row, she later recalled, "I left Richard a letter which said that we were destroying too many lives. We should part." Burton returned to Sybil and Taylor remained in Gstaad: "I was dying inside and trying to hide it from the children with all kinds of frenzied activity – games, picnics."

The parting didn't last. Richard called her out of the blue and told her he missed her. They arranged to have lunch at the Château de Chillon, the medieval castle overlooking Lake Geneva that inspired Lord Byron's poem *The Prisoner of Chillon*. Afterwards they met once or twice a week, and the affair resumed, but on a more gradual, less frenetic basis.

Richard was due to leave Switzerland to film *The VIPs* with Sophia Loren for MGM. Elizabeth announced she was interested in co-starring, and her old studio leapt at the chance of pairing the most newsworthy couple in the world. Loren was swapped for Taylor and filming began in London in December 1962.

The couple remained in London for the first half of 1963 while Burton filmed *Becket*. They then located to Mexico, where the actor was to star in John Huston's version of the Tennessee Williams play *The Night*

PAGE 80 *Every woman's worst nightmare: actress Gina Lollobrigida, and Taylor, wearing identical Dior dresses at a party to celebrate the Moscow Film Festival at the Kremlin, 1961. Elizabeth did not comment about the incident but Gina said, "It is a beautiful dress."*

PAGE 81 *Love on screen quickly turned to love off screen for the stars of* Cleopatra, *Taylor and Burton.*

LEFT *Taylor takes a break in the dressing room of the* Cleopatra *set. She held the Guinness World Record for most costume changes in a film, with 65 in* Cleopatra. *This was only overturned in 1996 when Madonna made 85 in* Evita.

RIGHT *There was obvious chemistry between Taylor and Burton on set.*

LEFT *Taylor at the door of her villa on the Via Appia, Rome, just after leaving hospital having had her stomach pumped following an overdose. There was never any question that she intended to kill herself – it was a cry for help following Burton initially choosing his wife over her.*

RIGHT, ABOVE *Taylor and Burton relax on the deck of a speedboat in 1962. A more compromising paparazzi shot of the two on this break confirmed to the world that the couple were more than just good friends.*

RIGHT *Elizabeth drinking a pint of bitter in a pub in London with Burton in 1962. The couple, still not divorced from their respective spouses although she was separated, were in London to film The VIPs.*

of the Iguana.

In the spring of 1963, Sybil Burton filed for divorce, citing abandonment and cruelty, and, according to her papers, the fact that "her husband had been in the constant company of another woman." Liz's marriage to Eddie Fisher also ended that spring, with the singer sarcastically adding, "I wouldn't stand in the way of this earth-shattering, world-shaking romance for anything in the world."

Elizabeth and Richard married on 15 March 1964, in the bridal suite on the eighth floor of the Ritz-Carlton Hotel in Montreal, Canada. Aged just 32 and about to marry husband number five, Taylor was, as one wag put it, "always the bride, never the bridesmaid", though she insisted Burton would be her final groom. "I didn't have butterflies for this one, because I knew beyond all doubt that it was right."

"You have both gone through great travail in your love for each other," the Unitarian minister told them. Nobody witnessing the ten-minute ceremony could have disagreed.

Later that day Burton was due on stage in *Hamlet* in Toronto. Afterwards he received six curtain calls. Richard stepped forward and announced, "I would like to quote from the play – act three, scene one: 'We will have no more marriages.'"

OPPOSITE *A still from* The VIPs. *Director Anthony Asquith originally wanted Sophia Loren in the roll of Frances Andros but Taylor, afraid of the effect Loren might have on Burton, persuaded him to give her the part.*

LEFT *Taylor and Burton finally married in 1964, on 15 April at the Ritz-Carlton Hotel, Montreal, Canada.*

6

Liz & Dick

"I never planned to acquire a lot of jewels or a lot of husbands."

RIGHT *Taylor wearing her famous necklace bearing the pearl "La Peregrina", a gift from Richard Burton for her thirty-seventh birthday. She based the setting of the pearl on a portrait of Mary Tudor, who wore it as a choker. Elizabeth often wore jewellery Burton had given her in her films, here in* A Little Night Music.

part from Eddie Fisher's appearance in *BUtterfield 8*, the only one of Elizabeth's husbands to star alongside her was of course Richard Burton. The two made 10 films together, 11 if you include Taylor's uncredited role as a courtesan in *Anne of the Thousand Days*.

Taylor once said of Burton as a co-star, "I think he made everyone want to do their best." Burton said of his wife in 1974, "I think she's one of the greatest screen actors." He would often recount how when he first acted with her, he complained to a mutual friend: "She doesn't do anything. What does she do?" The friend told him to go and look at the rushes the following day. Burton went to see them and came back impressed: "She was doing everything."

After his death, Taylor acknowledged that their completely different approaches – hers instinctive as always, his more rehearsed – benefited each other. "He very sweetly said that I taught him how to be a movie actor. He taught me how to be a better actress."

Their first joint venture after their wedding was a poetry and prose reading in aid of the American Musical and Dramatic Academy. Their self-deprecating humour clearly played a part in their choice of readings. Taylor, for example, read from Thomas Hardy's "The Ruined Maid":

And now you've gay bracelets and bright feathers three!
"Yes, that's how we dress when we're ruined," said she.

Burton replied with a reading from Eliot's "Portrait of a Lady", which begins with the quote:

Thou hast committed fornication
but that was in another country…

By now the Burtons – as they were jointly known – were the one of the most newsworthy couples on the planet and throughout the 1960s their every appearance, whether a lunch date or an airport arrival, guaranteed screaming fans and absolute mayhem. Richard at times found it hard to adjust to, but Elizabeth said, "I've had this all my life; you'll just have to get used to it."

BELOW LEFT *Tayor and Burton share a joke with Sammy Davis Junior in Davis's dressing room after his opening at New York's Copacabana nightclub, 30 April 1964.*

BELOW RIGHT *Burton makes a face at an unobserving Taylor, 1963. The pair had a volatile but tremendously loving relationship.*

A typical example was when they arrived in Boston, the last stop on Burton's *Hamlet* production before it transferred to Broadway. Three and a half thousand screaming fans waited at the airport in scenes reminiscent of The Beatles jetting in to New York a few months earlier. As the couple arrived at the Sheraton Plaza Hotel more fans invaded the lobby. Taylor was thrown against a wall as the crowd tore at her clothing and scratched her face. Burton had his hair pulled out and his suit torn as he fought to get to his wife, who was screaming "Back off!" at the horde.

Taylor's three children and Burton's daughter Kate often accompanied them on location or on their jet-set holidays to Mexico, Gstaad and elsewhere in Europe. Elizabeth was all too aware of the effect her much-married and peripatetic lifestyle must have had on Michael, Christopher and Liza. "My children are remarkable people," she told one interviewer in the 1960s, adding, "My life should have been murder for them. We've lived like gypsies and – well, there's the obvious fact that I've been married too many times."

With Elizabeth unable to have any more children, the couple adopted a daughter they named Maria Burton. Maria was born Petra Heisig in Germany in 1961 and was found through an advert placed by Taylor – via an intermediary – in a German magazine stating that a wealthy, childless, foreign couple (she was still married to Eddie Fisher at this point) wished

ABOVE *Elizabeth yet again shows her nurturing side as she tends to Richard Burton, sheltering from the hot Mexican sun under a folded newspaper on the set of* Night of the Iguana, *1963.*

LEFT *From her personal collection, Elizabeth Taylor, the mother, looking after her daughter, Liza Todd, and one of her sons on the set of Burton's* Becket *in August 1963.*

RIGHT *Again from her personal collection and perhaps even snapped by Taylor herself. Richard Burton gives one of her sons a ride on his horse in a break from filming* Becket *at Shepperton Studios, England.*

to adopt a baby. Petra's parents responded, and although the baby had a congenitally deformed hip and was malnourished, Taylor's first glimpse of the needy child brought out the best of her mothering instinct and she and Fisher decided to adopt her. The procedure wasn't finalized until 1964, by which time the actress was married to Burton.

Living and working together meant an often-bizarre way of life for the couple. Years later, the actress would recall, "On the set we would scream and blood would drip and brains would spill, and we'd get home and play with the kids, and go to bed and make love and then get around to studying our lines for the next day."

Three years after *Cleopatra*, Elizabeth recruited Mike Nichols to direct his first movie, based on Edward Albee's play *Who's Afraid of Virginia Woolf?*. The film explores the often-explosive relationship between George, an associate history professor played by Burton, and his hard-drinking wife Martha, played by Taylor.

Who's Afraid of Virginia Woolf? was nominated for 13 Oscars and has been the only film to be nominated in every eligible category at the Academy Awards. Taylor – who put on over 20 pounds (9kg), wore prosthetics under her eyes and chin, wore padding around her waist, dyed

BELOW *Taylor spent much time on set with her husband and was said to be loved by the crew and cast as she was so down-to-earth, no hiding in a trailer for her! Here the Broadway cast of* Hamlet, *in which Burton was playing the lead, sing "Happy Birthday" as she prepares to cut a cake, 1964.*

RIGHT *Taylor helps Burton learn his lines for the Oxford University Dramatic Society's production of* Dr Faustus. *Taylor appeared in the non-speaking role of Helen of Troy. She said, "I have never acted on stage before, so I'm starting the easy way. It's a marvellous opportunity." They appeared in nine performances alongside undergraduates and, like them, were not paid for their services.*

RIGHT *The couple drinking big glasses of beer on 5 April 1965 in front of the Hotel Post in Wallgau, Bavaria, Germany, where Richard Burton was filming the classic Cold War espionage thriller* The Spy Who Came in from the Cold. *As well as jewels, Burton is said to have given Taylor a love of bitter.*

LEFT, TOP AND BOTTOM *The role of Martha in the 1966 film* Who's Afraid of Virginia Woolf? *won Elizabeth her second best actress Oscar. She was, however, initially a controversial casting with many, including the writer, feeling Bette Davis would have made a better 50-something frump rather than "the most beautiful woman in the world". She proved critics wrong, gaining more than 20lbs (9kg) and aging rather effectively.*

OPPOSITE *Taylor and Burton in 1967, unafraid to show the world they were in love, three years into their marriage.*

her hair grey and, in her own words, "generally looked like a slob" – won her second Oscar for her role, and was gutted when Burton lost out to Paul Scofield for *A Man For All Seasons*. "I was so compelled by Richard," she said in a 2000 interview, "and why he didn't get a Best Actor Award makes me so angry – he was brilliant."

Although most of their joint films – *Boom*, *The Comedians*, *The Sandpiper* – are relatively forgettable now, astute negotiating resulted in the couple becoming among the highest earners in Hollywood at the time. Elizabeth

TOP LEFT *All of the photographs on this and the subsequent five pages are from a personal photo album Taylor gave to Michael Jackson, who subsequently left it, among other things, in the back of a chauffer-driven car in Germany, then told the driver to keep the items. They offer an unprecedented insight into Liz Taylor off duty.*

LEFT *On the set of* Reflections in a Golden Eye *with her co-star Marlon Brando. Brando's role was originally supposed to be played by Elizabeth's old friend Montgomery Clift but he died of a heart attack in July 1966.*

TOP RIGHT *Burton with Liza Todd (Elizabeth's daughter), Kate Burton (his own daughter) and Maria Burton (the couple's jointly adopted daughter), c.1967.*

RIGHT *Taylor on holiday c.1967 with Burton and their combined family.*

TOP LEFT *A candid shot of Richard Burton, perhaps taken by Taylor herself.*

LEFT *Elizabeth with one of Richard Burton's brothers, possibly in Mexico.*

LEFT & BELOW *More holiday photographs featuring Taylor, her children and Burton's extended family. Taylor and Burton seemed to be very successful at integrating their sprawling families.*

said, "I broke the sound barrier," when she got $1 million for *Cleopatra*; now she was routinely demanding it, earning another $1 million for *The Sandpiper* and $1.1 million for *Who's Afraid of Virginia Woolf?*. In addition the Burtons set up two companies that over the next eight years earned them more than $50 million, with royalties still added years later.

One joint venture that earned them absolutely nothing was their appearance at the Oxford Playhouse in 1966, when Burton repaid a favour to Nevill Coghill, who had directed him in a wartime production of *Measure for Measure* at Exeter College, Oxford. Richard agreed to star in a student production of *Dr Faustus* with Taylor playing the walk-on role of Helen of Troy. They stayed at the Randolph Hotel, next to the theatre, and despite the inevitable pandemonium at the press call, they had a fun time and hosted parties for the cast and students. Profits from this and the film of the same name went towards the construction of the 60-seater Burton-Taylor Studio, which still exists.

Having amassed millions of dollars, the couple had no compunction about spending it all. They bought a luxury yacht they named *Kalizma* after Kate, Liza and Maria, as well as a 10-passenger de Havilland jet for $1 million, which they called *Elizabeth*. The actress invested in art – buying works by Monet, Picasso, van Gogh, Renoir, Pissarro, Degas and Rembrandt. They even had "his and hers" Rolls-Royces: his silver, hers green. They stretched room service to its ultimate test by ordering from other countries – sausages from London's Fortnum and Mason and the famous chilli made by Chasen's restaurant in Beverley Hills, flown to them in Rome.

OPPOSITE TOP *Richard and Elizabeth in relaxed holiday mode in the sunshine by the pool.*

OPPOSITE BOTTOM LEFT & RIGHT, ABOVE LEFT & RIGHT *Shots from a house party with Marlon Brando. These photographs of all of them larking around offer an insight into the world they inhabited that is rarely seen by those on the outside.*

Their most famous purchases were of course jewels. For Valentine's Day 1969, Richard bought Elizabeth "La Peregrina", reckoned to be the most famous pearl in the world, which had once belonged to Mary Tudor, the eldest daughter of Henry VIII. He also bought her an emerald and diamond necklace with matching earrings, ring, brooch and bracelet that had belonged to the Grand Duchess Vladimir of Russia.

In 1968 the actor paid a staggering $305,000 for the Krupp diamond – equivalent to around $2 million today. Princess Margaret spotted it one day and said, "That's the most vulgar thing I've ever seen." In the same breath she asked if she could try it on. When Her Royal Highness stretched her hand out to admire it, Taylor retorted: "Not so vulgar now, is it?"

By the end of the Sixties the couple were regularly mixing with royalty. They dined with Margaret and her husband Lord Snowdon and visited the Duke and Duchess of Windsor at their Paris home in the Bois de Boulogne.

ABOVE *Burton and Taylor talking to Princess Margaret (as Michael Redgrave looks on) at the premiere of* The Taming of the Shrew, *Odeon Leicester Square, London, 28 February 1967. The trio were good friends, often dining together.*

RIGHT *The first outing of the "Taylor-Burton" diamond at a charity ball in honour of Princess Grace of Monaco (Grace Kelly)'s fortieth birthday in November 1969. When Burton bought it for $1.1 million it was the world's most expensive diamond.*

In 1972 Elizabeth turned 40. She had become a grandmother the previous year when Michael and his wife Beth had a daughter they named Leyla. Now, to celebrate the milestone, the Burtons flew family and friends to Budapest for a weekend of parties held at the Inter-Continental Hotel and attended by Princess Grace of Monaco, Michael Caine, Susannah York, Ringo Starr and David Niven.

In a press interview to mark her birthday, Taylor said, "I love my life and everything is going so well." As we have seen time and again in Elizabeth's life, the gap between reality and make-believe was, more often than not, huge. By 1972 very little was "going well" in her marriage, and Taylor the actress was merely playing "happy ever after".

BELOW *With Richard Burton and his sister, Cecelia James, on his birthday, posing with the CBE he had received earlier that day from the Queen at Buckingham Palace, 10 November 1970.*

RIGHT *Taylor at her fortieth birthday party. Around her neck is her present from Richard Burton – the Taj Mahal diamond. He joked at the time, "I would have liked to buy the Taj Mahal for Elizabeth but it would have cost too much to transport it."*

7

Divorce His...
Divorce Hers...

---

*"We really cannot keep away
from each other."*

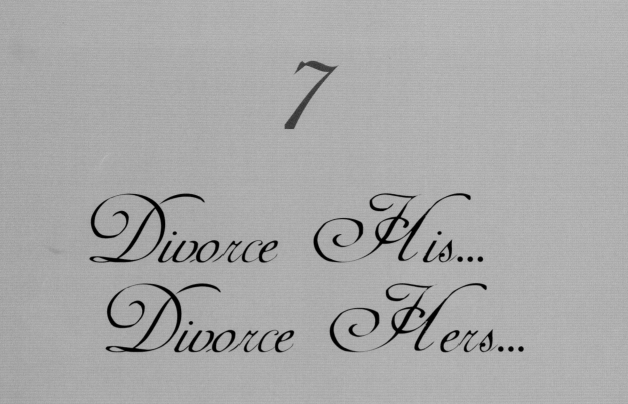

RIGHT *Taylor with David Bowie in Beverly Hills, 1975.*

On 4 July 1973, Elizabeth Taylor issued a statement: "I am convinced that it would be a good and constructive idea if Richard and I are separated for a while. Maybe we love each other too much – I never thought that was possible. But we have been in each other's pockets constantly, never being apart but for matters of life and death."

There was never anything bland in any of Elizabeth's statements and interviews, and this release was packed with emotion, intensity and drama. She went on to write: "I believe with all my heart that the separation will ultimately bring us back to where we should be – together." It ends with a plea: "Pray for us." The statement managed to knock the lengthy hearings of President Nixon's Watergate scandal off the front pages for a day or two.

Burton held his own press conference in New York. He told reporters, "It was jolly well bound to happen. You know when two very volatile people keep hacking at each other with fierce oratory, and then occasionally engage in a go of it with physical force, well it's like I said: it's bound to happen."

The same summer their final film, *Divorce His, Divorce Hers*, was released. It explored the conflicting emotions felt by a couple as their 18-year marriage disintegrates, and was a case of art imitating life.

There was a short-lived reunion at Sophia Loren's villa outside Rome while Burton was filming *The Voyage* with the Italian actress and Taylor was

BELOW *Taylor and Burton in the aptly titled* Divorce His, Divorce Hers. *Months later the couple announced they were to separate after nine years together.*

also in Italy to film *The Driver's Seat*. It was one of her worst movies, about a schizophrenic trying to find a man who would love her – and who ends up murdering her. As she herself said at the time, "How I get myself into these movies I'll never know."

That summer, President Kennedy's brother-in-law, the actor Peter Lawford, introduced Taylor to a used-car salesman called Henry Wynberg, and the two hit it off. Wynberg later recalled: "Before I knew where I was, I was in deep."

Then, in November, Elizabeth was rushed to the University of California Hospital with stomach pains. It turned out to be an ovarian cyst and as she prepared to be operated on, Burton hurried over from Rome to be with her, and Wynberg was shown the hospital door. Burton joked, "I can't bear the thought of losing the old girl," and any doubts she might have had about the reunion were hastily dispelled when he produced a 38-carat diamond necklace from Van Cleef and Arpels. A gleeful Taylor put it round her neck, saying, "You sure know how to win over a sick woman!"

The reunion was short-lived. On 26 April 1974, they announced their plans to end their ten-year marriage. Two months later Taylor was in court to hear the judge grant the divorce. She got to keep her jewels, valued at $5 million, her artwork, the yacht *Kalizma* and the house on the Mexican coast, as well as gaining custody of Maria.

ABOVE *The original caption that accompanied this photograph was "All's well that ends well, as someone in the theatrical trade once said. Richard Burton and his wife, Elizabeth Taylor, share laughter as she makes her first visit to the set of his film,* The Voyage *in Rome recently (3 January). She toasts his 'marriage' in the movie to Sophia Loren. After a recent brief disagreement and parting, Burton and Miss Taylor are together again." This reunion was short-lived: by the summer the couple had parted and Elizabeth was dating again.*

Taylor resumed her affair with Wynberg but still kept in regular touch with Burton. Then in August 1975 they met up again at the home of a mutual friend in Switzerland. There were hugs, kisses, tears and drunken fights, but six days later they announced they would remarry: "We really cannot keep away from each other."

Elizabeth's sixth wedding service took place on 10 October 1975, in Chobe Game Reserve, Botswana, before the district commissioner. They were surrounded by two hippos, a rhino and a cheetah.

The second marriage lasted ten months before they divorced, in Port-au-Prince, Haiti. "I love Richard Burton with every fibre of my soul," said Taylor, "but we can't be together – we are too mutually destructive."

That summer, Washington DC was celebrating the bicentenary of US independence. Taylor was invited to a White House reception for Queen Elizabeth II and, when she asked for an escort for the evening, it was arranged that she should be accompanied by Senator John Warner, chairman of the Bicentennial Administration.

Warner invited Elizabeth to see his 2,000-acre estate in Middleburg, Virginia. The two were smitten and, after Taylor fulfilled her commitment to star in the film version of *A Little Night Music* in Vienna, they became

OPPOSITE *Taylor with American used-car salesman Henry Wynberg. The couple started dating in the summer of 1973, but broke up again briefly when Elizabeth was reunited with Richard Burton. They soon reignited their relationship, only for it to end again with Taylor's second marriage to Burton.*

LEFT ABOVE *When Elizabeth was hospitalized Burton rushed to her side, despite the fact they were separated. However, months later they announced their divorce.*

engaged: Elizabeth looked forward to her new career as a politician's wife, as Warner looked forward to gaining a seat in the Senate. "John knows what he's going to do and I want to be by his side," she said. "I want to make my contribution to Washington."

The couple were married in a short Episcopalian ceremony on Warner's farm, attended only by a handful of friends and some of his employees. She later told reporters, "I feel at last I have come home to nest.... I just know my long search for roots is over."

Taylor was true to her word about her working for her new husband. She dutifully played the politician's wife for most of their six years together. Her only notable screen appearance during this time was in the 1980 movie *The Mirror Crack'd*, based on an Agatha Christie novel and starring her old friend Rock Hudson as well as her co-star from *National Velvet*, Angela Lansbury,

Elizabeth's marriage to John Warner was one of the low points of her life. Accustomed to being centre stage at all times, she at times felt relegated to a walk-on part in her husband's political campaigns. She admitted to feeling isolated and suffocated.

In her misery, she turned to food. Her weight ballooned and in addition she was drinking hard and taking prescription drugs. She became the butt

LEFT *Taylor follows her attorney from the courthouse of the small Swiss town of Saanen (near Gstaad) after the court granted her and actor Richard Burton an uncontested divorce on grounds of incompatibility, 26 June 1974. Burton was not present.*

ABOVE *Elizabeth laughs
uncontrollably on stage. A male
streaker had just run, completely naked,
across the stage before a world-wide
TV audience of 76 million people at
the Academy Awards in April 1974.
This picture captures perfectly her
infectious laugh.*

RIGHT *Mr and Mrs Burton once more.
"The Burtons" arrive at the Dorchester
hotel in London following a flight home
from South Africa where they were
married for the second time, November
1975.*

LEFT *Taylor in the anonymous role of Senator's wife attending a Red Cross Gray Ladies luncheon, 1 April 1979. She threw herself behind her husband and was, for some time, the perfect Senator's wife.*

BELOW *Taylor and her then fiancé John Warner with both of their families in Vienna, Austria, where Liz was filming A Little Night Music. Once again Taylor made every effort to integrate the man in her life with her family. From left, Michael Wilding Jnr (Taylor's son), Liza Todd (Taylor's Daughter), Mary Warner (Warner's daughter), Taylor, Warner, Jo Wilding (wife of Michael Wilding Jnr). The toddler is the child of Michael and Jo.*

of comedians' jokes, especially those of Joan Rivers, who had a stash of one-liners such as "Elizabeth loves to eat so much that she stands in front of her microwave and yells: Hurry!".

One thing that was indisputable was that Taylor could manage to diet and get into shape for most of her screen roles. In 1981 producer Zef Bufman suggested she should tour in a stage revival of *The Little Foxes*, the Lillian Hellman play that had been made into a successful film starring Bette Davis. Elizabeth leapt at the chance and immediately lost 20 pounds at a spa before the opening at the Kennedy Center in Washington in March 1981 in front of a star-studded audience headed by President Ronald Reagan.

Despite mixed reviews, the production moved to Broadway and then on to London. Meanwhile Taylor had moved to 700 Nimes Road, Bel-Air, Los Angeles, ahead of her separation from Warner on 21 December 1981.

The following spring, Elizabeth celebrated her fiftieth birthday in London and was thrilled when Richard agreed to attend her party. She was even more delighted when he agreed to co-star with her one final time in a New York production of *Private Lives*.

BELOW *Taylor having fun with Elton John and his customary large glasses backstage at the Spectrum Theater in Philadelphia, July 1976.*

LEFT *Taylor at a Wembley (England) studio with Stephen Sondheim, recording the songs for the film* A Little Night Music, *10 August 1976. Sondheim wrote the music and lyrics for the film.*

BELOW *President Ronald Reagan and first lady Nancy Reagan say hello to Taylor at the Kennedy Center in Washington after her performance in* The Little Foxes, *20 March 1981. The trio were well acquainted as Taylor's husband at the time was the Republican Senator John Warner.*

RIGHT *Despite being divorced, and both remarried, Taylor and Burton remained good friends. Here they are seen dancing at her fiftieth-birthday celebrations at Legends nightclub, London on 28 February 1982.*

By now Taylor was hopelessly addicted to booze and prescription drugs, which showed in her erratic stage performances. Her mood worsened when Burton jetted to Las Vegas to marry Sally Hay, a former production assistant for the BBC. Elizabeth's only comment was, "She can have him," before she announced her own engagement to Victor Luna, a Mexican lawyer whom she had been seeing off and on for the past year, though this proved to be just a stop-gap measure.

Elizabeth's health and emotional strength declined throughout the autumn of 1983 until her two sons, her daughter Liza, her brother Howard and long-time friend Roddy McDowall confronted her about her worrying behaviour. Finally in December of that year she entered the Betty Ford clinic for a seven-week stay.

She emerged looking far better than she had in years. She had lost weight and began to discover her former zest for life. Things were going well for her until 6 August 1984, when a telephone call shattered her world.

Elizabeth's publicist, Chen Sam, rang to tell her the devastating news that Richard had died suddenly the previous evening, having suffered a massive stroke at the age of 58. Taylor became hysterical and wouldn't stop crying.

It was made clear to her that her presence at Burton's funeral in Switzerland would be an unwelcome distraction. Instead she flew to Wales a week or so later to be with his family, having visited his grave in Céligny, Switzerland. Outside the modest home of Richard's sister, Hilda Owen, where Elizabeth stayed, a crowd of locals sang "We'll Keep a Welcome in the Hillside". Elizabeth told them, "I've come home."

OPPOSITE TOP *Taylor's Jewish faith was very important to her and she worked for Jewish charitable causes throughout her life. In December 1982 she visited Jerusalem and is seen here praying at the Wailing Wall.*

OPPOSITE BOTTOM *Taylor and Burton acted together for the final time in the Broadway production of Noel Coward's* Private Lives *in 1983. It ran for 63 performances.*

BELOW *Taylor was left devastated by Burton's death in August 1984 but didn't attend his funeral out of respect for his then wife, Sally. Instead she later visited the grave and also paid a visit to Burton's family, with whom she was always close, in Pontrhydyfen, Wales.*

8

Home Straight

"I don't think President Bush is doing anything at all about AIDS. In fact, I'm not sure he even knows how to spell AIDS."

RIGHT *Elizabeth Taylor – here at the 1985 Golden Globe Awards – relaunched herself in the mid-1980s as an activist and, thanks to rigorous dieting, re-established herself as one of the world's most glamorous women.*

*L*ess than a year after Richard's death, Elizabeth's eventful life took another twist. On 2 October 1985, her long-time friend and co-star Rock Hudson died from AIDS-related illness at his Beverley Hills home. The actor had at first claimed he was suffering from liver cancer, but in July that year admitted the truth while he was receiving treatment in a Paris hospital.

Hudson's suffering galvanized Taylor's nurturing side and she became focused on helping the struggle to find a cure for AIDS. "People were telling me not to get involved," she later admitted. "I received death threats and I was getting angrier and angrier."

She was one of the first celebrities to involve herself in HIV- and AIDS-related projects, organizing and hosting the first major fundraiser to help these causes, in 1984, before Hudson's condition was known. She co-founded the American Foundation for AIDS Reseach (AmfAR) in 1985 with Dr Michael Gottlieb and Dr Mathilde Krim. Krim later recalled, "In the early years of AIDS, the public homophobia was so intense it infuriated Elizabeth – it hurt her – and she was indignant."

The role played by such a high-profile figure in a cause like this cannot be underestimated. Her presence at charity galas, auctions and lectures contributed to keeping AmfAR's name in the headlines and helped raise $160 million by 2000.

Eight years later she also founded the Elizabeth Taylor AIDS Foundation (ETAF) to help provide critically needed support services for HIV and AIDS patients. The year before, in 1992, she was awarded a special Academy Award, the Jean Hersholt Humanitarian Award, to honour her work in this field.

Her work continued right to the end. For example, following Hurricane Katrina in 2006 she donated $40,000 to the NO/AIDS Task Force, a non-profit organization that gave help to those suffering from HIV and AIDS in the New Orleans area. Following her death, former President Bill Clinton and his wife Hillary commented on this humanitarian work: "Elizabeth's legacy will live on in many people around the world whose lives will be longer and better because of her work and the ongoing efforts of those she inspired."

In 2000, in recognition of her humanitarian work and her 60 years as an actress, Queen Elizabeth II made Taylor a Dame of the British Empire, and the actress travelled to Buckingham Palace to receive her award from the Queen. Another legendary showbiz figure, Julie Andrews, was also invested as a Dame at the same ceremony.

During these years Elizabeth's film career was in decline. She starred in occasional TV movies such as *Sweet Bird of Youth*, *There Must be a Pony* and *Poker Alice*, the latter with her old friend and onetime escort George Hamilton, and she twice played in the animated series *The Simpsons* – once as herself and once as baby Maggie Simpson, when she just uttered one word: "Daddy".

The last major high-grossing film she was involved in was *The Flintstones*, in which she played Fred's nagging mother-in-law, Pearl Slaghoople. Then, after a gap of seven years, she starred in *These Old Broads* alongside Shirley MacLaine, Joan Collins and Debbie Reynolds.

In 2007, acting and her care for AIDS research came together when she acted on stage one final time, playing opposite James Earl Jones in a benefit performance of the A.R. Gurney play *Love Letters*. Five hundred people paid $2,500 per head to attend, raising more than $1 million for her AIDS foundation. The event took place against the backdrop of that year's strike by the Writers Guild of America. Rather than cross their picket line, Taylor asked if they would consider a one-night dispensation. Such was the respect

OPPOSITE *Taylor at the 1985 Golden Globe Awards with Liza Minnelli and Rock Hudson – the latter visibly ill. His death, later that year, of an AIDS-related disease inspired Elizabeth in her crusade to find a cure.*

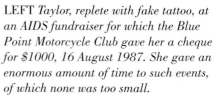

LEFT *Taylor, replete with fake tattoo, at an AIDS fundraiser for which the Blue Point Motorcycle Club gave her a cheque for $1000, 16 August 1987. She gave an enormous amount of time to such events, of which none was too small.*

ABOVE *Speaking to the crowd at Wembley Stadium at the tribute concert for the late Freddie Mercury on 20 April 1992. Mercury, the lead singer of the band Queen, died of AIDS in 1991.*

LEFT *A serious Taylor testifying at a meeting of the Sub Committee of Labor, Health, Human Services, Education and related agencies regarding AIDS, Washington DC.*

for her and the cause that the strikers agreed not to picket the Paramount Pictures lot that night.

Taylor also used her skills in another direction – as a businesswoman. No self-respecting celebrity is without their own fragrance, but Taylor's has stood the test of time. Although it was launched over 20 years ago, her "White Diamond" perfume, manufactured by Elizabeth Arden, remains the world's best-selling fragrance, with global sales reaching $61.3 million in 2010.

Elizabeth was one of the first stars to involve herself in the business, and some of her subsequent perfumes, including "Diamonds and Emeralds", "Diamonds and Rubies" and "Black Pearls", still sell well, with sales of $76.9 million in 2010. The actress worked hard to promote her fragrances and even agreed to host a private tea party for the first 150 customers who bought a $300-an-ounce limited edition of "White Diamonds". Her first fragrance,

RIGHT *At the 1993 Academy Awards Elizabeth was awarded a special humanitarian Oscar for her work in the cause of the fight against HIV/AIDS.*

OPPOSITE *Arriving at a benefit for her own AIDS foundation in 2007. She raised over $1 million that night alone, and over $100 million in her lifetime to fight the disease.*

LEFT, TOP *The newly married Taylor and Fortensky, with Michael Caine (left) and Elton John (right) at a charity reopening of the refurbished Mirabelle restaurant in London's Mayfair. The couple divorced five years later, with his family saying he simply didn't want to be "Mr Elizabeth Taylor" any more. Taylor's life was very different to that of a construction worker he was used to.*

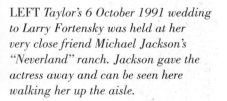

LEFT *Taylor's 6 October 1991 wedding to Larry Fortensky was held at her very close friend Michael Jackson's "Neverland" ranch. Jackson gave the actress away and can be seen here walking her up the aisle.*

"Passion", was released in 1987 and her last one, "Violet Eyes", came out in 2010. In all she launched ten fragrances, and once said, "I think [perfume] is more than just an accessory for a woman. It's part of her aura. I wear it even when I'm alone."

After a further spell in rehab in the late 1980s, Taylor emerged once again looking fit and healthy, and this time with a new man in her life. Larry Fortensky was a construction worker, 20 years her junior, who had checked into the Betty Ford Clinic after a drink-driving conviction.

Elizabeth and Larry, husband number eight, were married on 6 October 1991 on Michael Jackson's "Neverland" ranch, watched by a star-studded gathering including Liza Minnelli, Eddie Murphy, Nancy Reagan and Macaulay Culkin. Elizabeth wore a £25,000 yellow wedding dress, a gift from the designer Valentino, and the couple toasted each other with mineral water.

Although Fortensky remained loyal to Elizabeth, he found it difficult to integrate with her friends and grew tired of being Mr Elizabeth Taylor. They divorced in October 1996 and, thanks to a pre-nuptial agreement, he walked away with $1 million of her fortune, which even then was estimated at over $1 billion.

Taylor's friendship with Michael Jackson continued off and on for the rest of their lives. In 1997 he presented her with a song, "Elizabeth, I Love You", which he performed on her sixty-fifth birthday. She was a vocal supporter of him in his 2005 trial for allegedly sexually abusing a child, and attended his private funeral in September 2009.

Elizabeth Taylor's final years were a constant battle against ill health. She survived an operation on a benign brain tumour in 1997, then two years later fell and fractured her back, exacerbating the back problems she had suffered from since a riding accident while filming *National Velvet*.

On 30 May 2006 she appeared on *Larry King Live* to deny claims that she was suffering from Alzheimer's disease and close to death. During her final years she was confined to a wheelchair, having developed osteoporosis, though it failed to deter her spirit and zest for life. In 2010 she returned to her beloved England one last time to attend a gala at Buckingham Palace hosted by Prince Charles to mark the sixtieth anniversary of the Royal Welsh College of Music and Drama and to see a bust of Richard Burton that will stand in a new theatre to be named after him.

In February 2011 it was announced that Taylor had been admitted into Cedars-Sinai Medical Center in Los Angeles with congestive heart failure. She remained there until she passed away at the age of 79 on 23 March, surrounded by her four children, ten grandchildren and four great-grandchildren.

At her funeral the following day, at the Forest Lawn Memorial Park, Taylor had one last mischievous trick up her sleeve. Famed for her tardy timekeeping, she asked to arrive 15 minutes after the service had begun and for someone to say, "She even wanted to be late for her own funeral." She also asked to be buried with the last letter Richard Burton wrote to her, in which he told her he wanted "to come home". The romance that began under sultry summer skies half a century earlier was now finally over, its two passionate protagonists finally at peace.

Elizabeth Taylor was so many things – a wife and mother, an actress, a businesswoman and a humanitarian. She would be the first to admit she wasn't always a success in any of those areas, but somehow she managed to transcend them all and become completely unassailable, almost beyond our mere mortal comprehension.

Asked how she would like to be remembered on her tombstone, Taylor said, "Here lies Elizabeth. She hated being called Liz. But she lived." And lived she most certainly did.

LEFT *Taylor launching her first perfume, "Passion", in 1987. She was one of the first celebrities to embrace the concept of themselves as a brand and made much of her fortune from her business ventures rather than her acting.*

ABOVE *Taylor accompanied by her friend Michael Jackson at her sixty-fifth birthday party at Pantagers Theater, Hollywood. Jackson wrote and performed a song for the occasion –* "Elizabeth, I Love You".

LEFT *A publicity shot for* These Old Broads, *a 2001 TV movie. From left to right: Debbie Reynolds, Elizabeth Taylor, Shirley MacLaine and Joan Collins. It was written by Carrie Fisher, the daughter of Eddie Fisher and Debbie Reynolds, who was two when her father left her mother for Taylor.*

RIGHT *In 1999 Taylor was awarded the BAFTA Fellowship – "in recognition of outstanding achievement in the art forms of the moving image".*

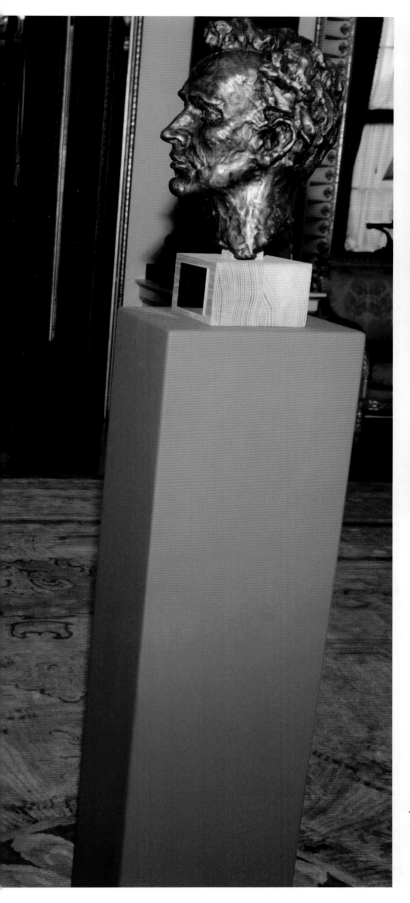

ABOVE *Taylor after the ceremony at which she was created a Dame of the British Empire in 2000.*

LEFT *In April 2010, although very frail, Elizabeth attended a reception at Buckingham Palace with Price Charles to celebrate the Royal Welsh College's silver jubilee, which included the unveiling of a bust of the love of her life, Richard Burton.*

RIGHT *Tributes left by fans at the Elizabeth Taylor Star on the Hollywood Walk of Fame, Los Angeles, 23 March 2011. She was buried the next day at a private family funeral at the Forest Lawn Memorial Park, Glendale, California – the same cemetery that Michael Jackson is buried in.*

FILMOGRAPHY

1942
There's One Born Every Minute
Plays: Gloria Twine
Director: Harold Young

1943
Lassie Come Home
Plays: Priscilla
Director: Fred Wilcox

1944
Jane Eyre
Plays: Helen Burns
Director: Robert Stevenson

1944
The White Cliffs of Dover
Plays: Betsy
Director: Clarence Brown

1944
National Velvet
Plays: Velvet Brown
Director: Clarence Brown

1946
Courage of Lassie
Plays: Katherine Eleanor
  Merrick
Director: Fred Wilcox

1947
Cynthia
Plays: Cynthia Bishop
Director: Robert Z. Leonard

1947
Life with Father
Plays: Mary Skinner
Director: Michael Curtiz

1948
A Date with Judy
Plays: Carol Pringle
Director: Richard Thorpe

1948
Julia Misbehaves
Plays: Susan Packett
Director: Jack Conway

1949
Little Women
Plays: Amy
Director: Mervyn LeRoy

1949
Conspirator
Plays: Melinda Greyton
Director: Victor Saville

1950
Father of the Bride
Plays: Kay Banks
Director: Vincente Minnelli

1950
The Big Hangover
Plays: Mary Belney
Director: Norman Krasna

1951
Father's Little Dividend
Plays: Kay Dunstan
Director: Vincente Minnelli

1951
A Place in the Sun
Plays: Angela Vickers
Director: George Stevens

1951
Quo Vadis?
Plays: Christian prisoner in
arena (uncredited)
Director: Mervyn LeRoy

1952
Love Is Better Than Ever
Plays: Anastasia "Stacie"
  Macaboy
Director: Stanley Donen

1952
Ivanhoe
Plays: Rebecca
Director: Richard Thorpe

1953
The Girl Who Had Everything
Plays: Jean Latimer
Director: Richard Thorpe

1954
Rhapsody
Plays: Louise Durant
Director: Richard Thorpe

1954
Elephant Walk
Plays: Ruth Wiley
Director: William Dieterle

1954
Beau Brummell
Plays: Lady Patricia Belham
Director: Curtis Bernhardt

1954
The Last Time I Saw Paris
Plays: Helen Ellisworth
Director: Richard Brooks

1956
Giant
Plays: Leslie Lynnton Benedict
Director: George Stevens

1957
Raintree County
Plays: Susanna Drake
Director: Edward Dmytryk
• Nominated – Academy Award
for Best Actress

1958
Cat on a Hot Tin Roof
Plays: Maggie the Cat
Director: Richard Brooks
• Nominated – Academy Award
for Best Actress

1959
Suddenly, Last Summer
Plays: Catherine Holly
Director: Joseph L Mankiewicz
• Nominated – Academy Award
for Best Actress

1960
Scent of Mystery (aka *Holiday
in Spain*)
Plays: The Real Sally
  (uncredited)
Director: Michael Anderson

1960
BUtterfield 8
Plays: Gloria Wandrous
Director: Daniel Mann
• Won – Academy Award for
Best Actress

1963
Cleopatra
Plays: Cleopatra
Director: Joseph L Mankiewicz

1963
The VIPs
Plays: Frances Andros
Director: Anthony Asquith

1965
The Sandpiper
Plays: Laura Reynolds
Director: Vincente Minnelli

1966
Who's Afraid of Virginia Woolf?
Plays: Martha
Director: Mike Nichols
• Won – Academy Award for
Best Actress

1967
The Taming of the Shrew
Plays: Katharina
Director: Franco Zeffirelli

1967
Doctor Faustus
Plays: Helen of Troy
Director: Richard Burton and
  Neville Coghill

1967
Reflections in a Golden Eye
Plays: Leonora Penderton
Director: John Huston

1967
The Comedians
Plays: Martha Pineda
Director: Peter Glenville

1968
Boom!
Plays: Flora "Sissy" Goforth
Director: Joseph Losey

1968
Secret Ceremony
Plays: Lenora
Director: Joseph Losey

1969
Anne of the Thousand Days
Plays: courtesan (uncredited)
Director: Charles Jarrott
[not listed in AD book]

1970
The Only Game in Town
Plays: Fran Walker
Director: George Stevens

1972
X,Y, and Zee (aka *Zee & Co.*)
Plays: Zee Blakely
Director: Brian G Hutton

1972
Under Milk Wood
Plays: Rosie Probert
Director: Andrew Sinclair

1972
Hammersmith Is Out
Plays: Jimmie Jean Jackson
Director: Peter Ustinov
• Silver Bear for Best Actress

1973
Night Watch
Plays: Ellen Wheeler
Director: Brian G Hutton

1973
Ash Wednesday
Plays: Barbara Sawyer
Director: Larry Peerce

1974
Identikit (aka *The Driver's Seat*)
Plays: Lise
Director: Guiseppe Patroni
  Griffi

1974
That's Entertainment!
Plays: herself (co-host)
Director: n/a. *That's
Entertainment!* is a compilation
film released by Metro-Goldwyn-
Mayer to celebrate its fiftieth
anniversary. Taylor narrates.

1976
The Blue Bird
Plays: Queen of Light/Mother/
Witch/Maternal Love
Director: George Cukor

1977
A Little Night Music
Plays: Desiree Armfeldt
Director: Harold Prince

1979
Winter Kills
Plays: Lola Comante
  (uncredited)
Director: William Richert

1980
The Mirror Crack'd
Plays: Marina Rudd
Director: Guy Hamilton

1981
Genocide
Plays: narrator
Director: Arnold Schwartzman

1988
Young Toscanini (aka *Il Giovane
  Toscanini*)
Plays: Nadina Bulichoff
Director: Franco Zeffirelli

1994
The Flintstones
Plays: Pearl Slaghoople
Director: Brian Levant

FILMS/MINI-SERIES FOR TELEVISION

1970
TV series, 1 episode
Here's Lucy
Plays: herself
Director: n/a.
Perhaps the most famous
episode was one from 1970
in which Richard Burton and
Elizabeth Taylor guest star in a
storyline involving their famous
diamond, which becomes stuck
on Lucy (Lucille Ball)'s finger.

1973
TV movie – shown as two-parter
on US television
Divorce His, Divorce Hers
Plays: Jane Reynolds
Director: Waris Hussein

1976
TV movie distributed by ABC
Victory at Entebbe
Plays: Edra Vilonfsky
Director: Marvin J Chomsky

1978
TV movie
Return Engagement
Plays: Dr Emily Loomis
Director: Joseph Hardy

1981
TV series – US soap opera
(ABC), three episodes, dated 16,
17, 18/11/1981
General Hospital
Plays: Helena Cassadine #1
Director: Phil Sogard/Alan Pultz

1983
TV movie
Between Friends
Plays: Deborah Shapiro
Director: Lou Antonio

1984
TV series, one episode
("Intimate Strangers")
Hotel
Plays: Katherine Cole
Director: Vincent McEveety

1984
TV series
All My Children
Plays: boardmember at the
  chateau
Director: ?

1985
TV movie
Malice in Wonderland
Plays: Louella Parsons
Director: Gus Trikonis

1985
TV mini-series, episode 1.5
North and South
Plays: Madame Conti
Director: Richard T Heffron

1986
TV movie
There Must Be a Pony
Plays: Marguerite Sydney
Director: Joseph Sargent

1987
TV movie
Poker Alice
Plays: Alice Moffit
Director: Arthur Alice
  Seidelman

1989
TV movie
Sweet Bird of Youth
Plays: Alexandra Del Lago
Director: Nicolas Roeg

1992
TV series, episode: "Lisa's First
  Word"
The Simpsons
Plays: Maggie Simpson (voice)
Director: Mark Kirkland

1992
Animated TV series – US TBS
*Captain Planet and the
  Planeteers*
Plays: Mrs Andrews (voice)
Director: ?

1993
TV series
The Simpsons
Plays: herself
Director: ?

2001
TV movie
These Old Broads
Plays: Beryl Mason
Director: Matthew Diamond

2001
TV series one episode ("God's Girlfriend")
God, the Devil and Bob
Plays: Sarah (voice)
Director: Dan Fausett

AWARDS AND HONOURS

1958
Academy Award nomination, Best Actress for her role as Maggie Pollitt in *Cat on a Hot Tin Roof*
BAFTA nomination, Best Foreign Actress for her role as Maggie Pollitt in *Cat on a Hot Tin Roof*

1959
Academy Award nomination, Best Actress for her role as Catherine Holly in *Suddenly, Last Summer*
Golden Globe Award, Best Actress in a Motion Picture – Drama – for her role as Catherine Holly in *Suddenly, Last Summer*

1960
Academy Award, Best Actress for her role as Gloria Wandrous in *BUtterfield 8*
Golden Globe Award nomination, Best Actress in a Motion Picture – Drama – for her role as Gloria Wandrous in *BUtterfield 8*

1966
Academy Award, Best Actress for her role as Martha in *Who's Afraid of Virginia Woolf?*
BAFTA British Film Academy Award, Best British Actress for her role as Martha in *Who's Afraid of Virginia Woolf?*
Golden Globe Award nomination, Best Actress in a Motion Picture – Drama – for her role as Martha in *Who's Afraid of Virginia Woolf?*
National Board of Review Award, Best Actress for her role as Martha in *Who's Afraid of Virginia Woolf?*
New York Film Critics Circle Award, Best Actress for her role as Martha in *Who's Afraid of Virginia Woolf?*
Golden Globe Award, Henrietta Award (World Film Favorites) – Nominated

1968
BAFTA nomination, Best British Actress for her role as Katharina in *The Taming of the Shrew*
BAMBI Award (Europe's Media Award) – Hubert Korda Media

1969
Golden Globe, Henrietta Award (World Film Favorites) – nominated

1972
Berlin International Film Festival, Silver Bear for Best Actress for her role as Jimmie Jean Jackson in *Hammersmith Is Out*
David di Donatello Award, Best Foreign Actress (Migliore Attrice Straniero) for her role as Zee Blakeley in *Zee and Co.*

1974
Golden Globe Award nomination, Best Actress in a Motion Picture – Drama – for her role as Barbara Sawyer in *Ash Wednesday*
Golden Globe Award, Henrietta Award (World Film Favorites)

1977
Hasty Pudding Theatricals (Harvard University) – Woman of the Year

1980
Simon Wiesenthal Distinguished Service Award

1981
Special Outer Critics Circle Award; Debut – *The Little Foxes*
Tony Award nomination, Best Actress (Play) – *The Little Foxes*

1985
Cecil B. DeMille Award – Hollywood Foreign Press (Golden Globe Awards)
Commandeur De l'Ordre des Arts et des Lettres – France
Women in Film Crystal Award

1986
Film Society of Lincoln Center – Gala Tribute

1988
The Legion d'Honneur for her work with AmfAR – France

1992
The Prince of Asturias Award for her work with AmfAR – Spain

1993
AFI Life Achievement Award
Jean Hersholt Humanitarian Award, Academy of Motion Picture Arts & Sciences

1998
Screen Actors Guild – Life Achievement Award

1999
BAFTA Fellowship Award

2000
Dame of the British Empire – United Kingdom
GLAAD Vanguard Award
Marian Anderson Award

2001
Presidential Citizens Medal

2002
Kennedy Center Honor

2005
BAFTA/LA Cunard Britannia Award for Artistic Excellence in International Entertainment

BIBLIOGRAPHY

AMBURN, Ellis — *Elizabeth Taylor* — Harper Collins

BRAGG, Melvyn — *Rich; The Life of Richard Burton* — Hodder & Stoughton

CHRISTOPHER, James — *Elizabeth Taylor – The Illustrated Biography* — Andre Deutsch

KASHNER, Sam — *Furious Love – Elizabeth Taylor, Richard Burton and the Marriage of the Century* — Harper Collins

KELLY, Kitty — *Elizabeth Taylor – The Last Star* — Michael Joseph

LEONARD, Maurice — *Montgomery Clift* — Hodder & Stoughton

SPOTO, Donald — *Elizabeth Taylor* — Little, Brown and Co

TARABORELLI, J.Randy — *Elizabeth* — Sidgwick & Jackson

TAYLOR, Elizabeth — *Elizabeth Taylor – An Informal Memoir* — Harper & Row

TAYLOR, Elizabeth — *My Love Affair With Jewelry* — Simon & Schuster

PICTURE CREDITS

The publishers would like to thank the following sources for their kind permission to reproduce the pictures in this book.

Key: t = top, b = bottom, c = centre, l = left and r = right

Corbis: /Bettmann: 24, 38, 43, 46, 47, 53 b, 56, 62 c, 65, 73, 77, 83, 106, 111, 115 t, 16-17, 48-49, 132-133, /Condé Nast Archive: 107, /Mario Anzuoni/Reuters: 130, /Norman Parkinson/Sygma: 89, /Phil Ramey/Sygma: 131 c, /Neal Preston: 9 r, 128 t, /Steve Starr: 129, /Sunset Boulevard: 81, /Underwood & Underwood: 86

Getty Images: 7, 31 t, 42, 45, 49 b, 52, 63, 75, 78, 82, 85 t, 85 b, 91, 109, 112, 115 b, 118 t, /AFP: 136-7, /Gamma-Keystone: 79, 84, /Gamma-Rapho: 12, 14, 15, 23, 27 t, 35, 36, 55, 64, /NY Daily News: 66 c, 69, 126-127, /Popperfoto: 29, 49 t, /Redferns: 11, /Time & Life Pictures: 39, 44 t, 66 b, 94, 116 t, 120 b, 143, /Wireimage: 5

InterTOPICS Gmbh: 9 l, 92, 93, 98 t, 98 b, 99 t, 99 b, 100 t, 100 b, 101 t, 101 b, 102 t, 102 bl, 102 br, 103 l, 103 r

Picture-Desk: /The Kobal Collection: 20, 21, 22, /The Kobal Collection/Columbia: 68, /The Kobal Collection/MGM: 8, 26, 27 b, 31 b, 37, 70-71, /The Kobal Collection/MGM/Frank Shugrue: 60, /The Kobal Collection/Paramount/A.L. 'Whitey' Schafer: 44 b, /The Kobal Collection/Warner Bros: 96 t, 96 c, /The Kobal Collection/World Film Services: 110

Press Association Images: 104, 119, 131 t, /AP Photo: 25, 32, 33, 51, 57, 58, 61, 80, 90 l, 114, 116 b, /AP Photo/Dennis Cook: 118 b, /AP Photo/Maestri: 105, /AP Photo/David Nutter: 117, /AP Photo/Lennox McLendon: 123, /AP Photo/Max Nash: 120 t, /AP Photo/Chris Pizzello: 134 t, /AP Photo/Sansen: 95 b, /Fiona Hanson: 137, /Landov: 28, 59

Rex Features: 87, 90 r, /Associated Newspaper: 113, /Brendan Beirne: 121, /Stuart Clarke: 13, /Everett Collection: 30, 51, 53 t, 62 t, 67, 74, 134 b, /Bruce Fleming: 97, /Peter Heimsath: 128 c, /Keystone USA-Zuma: 138-139, /Sipa Press: 124, /Snap: 20 , 40, 76, /Michael Ward: 95 t, /Richard Young: 135

Every effort has been made to acknowledge correctly and contact the source and/or copyright holder of each picture and Carlton Books Limited apologises for any unintentional errors or omissions, which will be corrected in future editions of this book

BOCA RATON PUBLIC LIBRARY, FLORIDA

3 3656 0596582 3

92 Taylor
Lloyd, Ian, 1960-
Elizabeth Taylor, 1932-2011

JUL   2012